# *Knowing Writers*

# *Knowing Writers*

## Essays and Reviews

## Walter Cummins

───────────────

Del Sol Press
Washington, D.C.

Knowing Writers: Essays and Reviews
by Walter Cummins

Published by Del Sol Press
Washington, D.C.

First printing 2017

Cover: Walter Cummins

Printed in the United States of America

ISBN 9780692974049

For all the writers I've known
and those I wish I knew

# Acknowledgements

Earlier verions of these essays and reviews appeared in the following magazines:

*Arts and Letters*:"Kennedy and Kerrigan in Copenhagen"
*da Cunha*: "Gaytys and Dangs: Echoing George P. Elliott"
*The Literary Review*: "The Invertiscope: Multiple Realities in *Mount Terminus*"; "Greg Herriges, *JD: A Memoir of a Time and a Journey*"; Review of Linda Lappin, *The Etruscan*; Review of Linda Lappin, *Katherine's Wish*
*New Letters*: "Roth's Complaint"
*Perigee*: "Knowing Vance Bourjaily"; "Rabbit's Door"; "Books Everywhere"
*PIF*: "*Riding the Dog: A Look Back at America* by Thomas E. Kennedy"
*Potpourri*: "Rooms of Their Lives: Where British Authors Lived and Wrote"
*Queen Mob's Teahouse*: "Existentialism and Story Writing"
*Serving House Journal*: "Knowing Writers; Richard E. Kim's *The Martyred*: Fleeting Fame"; "Deciphering and Creating Identities: Peter Selgin, *The Inventors*"; "Christopher Meredith, *The Book of Idiots*"; Review of Linda Lappin, *Signatures in Stone*; "Will Computers Write Literary Fiction"
*South 85*: "Creative Minds and Mental States"
*Zeteo*: "Americans' Anger: H. L. Hix"; "The Worlds of the Ordinary: Chris Arthur's *On the Shoreline of Knowledge: Irish Wanderings*"; "Biblical Uncertainties"

# Contents

# Knowing Writers

The first writer I ever knew may have been the history teacher I had my sophomore year in high school—a wide-hipped, thick-lipped man, around thirty, with short colorless hair and pale eyes wobbling behind pink-framed glasses, who wrote stories about a character named Philip Wedge. I know this because he took class time to read his latest to us.

But I don't recall what my teacher's stories were about or if they were any good, something I had no ability to judge at age fifteen. He probably was violating some school rule by inflicting them on us instead of bringing us up to speed on the German Peasants' Revolt of 1524 or the Treaty of Utrecht. I do recall that I didn't look forward to his stories—unlike a red-haired young woman a class behind mine who eloped with the Wedge-writer in must have been a much graver rule violation. He was fired in public outrage, and the couple fled town. I heard about this when I was in college and should have taken it as a cautionary tale that writers—even the unsuccessful ones—live on the edge.

When a college freshman at Rutgers, I learned one of my senior fraternity brothers had published a number of stories in the campus literary magazine and was considered very talented, though he took a real job and never did pursue his talent after graduation. Two people I knew casually during my undergraduate years did fulfill theirs. Mark Musa, who went on to a PhD in Italian, began translating Dante under the tutelage of John Ciardi. Ciardi, then the entire creative writing faculty, was famous for his version of *The Inferno*.

Ciardi also taught a young man named Norman Fruchter, who published a novel called *Coat Upon a Stick* when he was only twenty-five. Ciardi praised it glowingly in *The Saturday Review*: "Which is to say Fruchter has taken on nothing less than the ultimate tragic themes. Astonishingly, he has been equal to them. If he can go on from this first novel, there will be few in his generation to stand as his equals." (Fruchter did produce another novel eight years later, but most of his career has been as a social activist and academic.) For a year, when I was a senior and he a sophomore, Fruchter and I co-edited the college literary magazine, though then, while we sat around a table shuffling submissions, I had no inkling of his astonishing talent. When, later, I bought his book, I still couldn't connect its skill with the slight, young-looking man who wrote it.

But I fantasized being a real writer too, with only a vague idea of what that meant. Back in those days when I was signing up for lit courses, authors mattered, still enjoying a post-Romantic aura of significance. While not spoken in awe, their names commanded respect. Even non-English majors knew important books they should have read and claimed they eventually wanted to read. Some actually did, and it was through them I heard about, say, John Fowles and Par Lagerkvist.

Occasionally, writers came to campus. Robert Frost made an annual appearance during which, from one visit to the next, he made contradictory statements about the sources and meanings of his famous poems. Was he toying with us for his fee? One of my fraternity brothers—the talented writer—was given the "privilege" of meeting James T.

Farrell at the train station. The faculty hosts who avoided the station meeting must have been toying with my friend, who had the job of sobering up Farrell to a state where he could stand in front of an audience and speak coherently. Still, I thought being a writer was special. I had read and liked Farrell's Studs Lonigan novels, which sat, along with his story collections, on my shelf of Signet paperbacks. Besides, writers drank. Everybody knew that.

It wasn't until my junior year that I worked up the nerve to enroll in a creative writing course—with excessive angst. Though I had been a reporter for the campus newspaper since a freshman and was turning out short so-called humor pieces, fiction writing was to my mind an elevation to a much higher literary level. Was I being presumptuous? Would I humiliate myself? (Actually, I did at one point, reading out loud what I had written as a horror story and having my classmates crack up, the laughter louder with each sentence, the instructor along with the others, unable to keep a straight face.)

John Ciardi was off translating Dante's *Purgatorio* the semester I signed up. (It wasn't till years later, when I was teaching, that I met him in person.) I don't even recall the name of his replacement, a man on leave from another university. I hadn't thought to look him up. Despite my day of well-deserved ridicule, I came out with a B. But what else can you give a student who turns in the minimum word count, shows up for every class, and tries his best, however limited that best might be?

Eventually, a couple of my stories ended up in the campus literary magazine, my copies of which were tossed long ago in the triage of packing for one of many moves, the stories themselves forgotten. Did Fruchter approve of them? Would it matter? We usually were desperate to fill pages.

After graduation I took a job as an advertising-sales promotion trainee, dragging my very young then-wife to a snowbound company town with only the haziest conception of my future. I had to earn a living because that's what people do. Certainly, no one encouraged me to pursue fiction writing, but I found I couldn't stop. Back then, with a much steadier hand than now, while neighbors barbecued, I fixed blank paper in a clipboard and filled sheets with words, eventually typing versions of those stories on a manual Smith-Corona, aching to make them better, ashamed of my limitations, wondering if a virtual classroom were laughing behind my back.

By coincidence, one of my fellow trainees—a man who had dropped out of a PhD program at Indiana because he couldn't contemplate living on an academic salary—was married to the daughter of Granville Hicks. Hicks, then a well-known critic, wrote a Literary Horizons column for *The Saturday Review*—in a further coincidence, the same weekly that contained John Ciardi's regular column, one of which exalted Fruchter.

Hicks was teaching a community writing workshop in Grafton, New York, the village in which he lived near the Vermont line. I signed up and once a week drove an hour back and forth to a room in which I was the kid, just twenty-two, sitting in a circle among retired women missionaries working on their memoirs and schoolteachers turning out pedantic essays. Hicks, a kind, soft-spoken man, tolerated my stories, offering a few words of praise about a passage or a sentence. At the time, I hadn't known he was a former member of the Communist Party, fired from college teaching for being a Red. Instead of subverting me, he provided enough incentive for me to keep writing and keep showing up for group sessions, even on treacherous roads after winter storms.

By the time I was engaged in the Hicks workshop, I had seen far enough into my future to know I didn't want to become a corporate advertising-sales executive. Instead, I decided to apply to graduate schools, a path that had never crossed my undergraduate mind, as much as I liked reading and writing. But first I had to complete military service, a given for males of my generation, manipulating my way to just six months active duty in the National Guard by lying that I wanted to be an officer, a status with as little appeal as being an executive. That meant infantry training despite my inability to shoot straight or complete a round of morning pull-ups. Basic training verified that I had even less aptitude for a military career than I did for a corporate one. What is there but teaching and writing for a person too bored to manage budgets and too inept to lead troops into combat?

Halfway through my infantry days, my mediocre typing skills got me the role as company clerk, sitting behind a desk to peck out morning reports while my company-mates trudged through mud, weighted down by knapsacks. The role was an omen of future decades seated with fingers on a keyboard, slogging through the muck in my mind.

Back on civvy street, I applied to grad schools and found a job as a technical editor with a small technical manual firm, using a skill gained during my abortive corporate training. My then-wife was finishing college. We found a one-room basement apartment in Brooklyn Heights, not far from where Hart Crane had written *The*

*Bridge*, just a single BMT stop from my workplace, itself a much larger, shabby one-room space stuffed with desks, easels, and filing cabinets. Saturday mornings, anticipating grad school, I took a PhD German translation course at NYU, and for one evening a week I signed up for a non-credit fiction class at the New School.

That's where I really changed my life, choosing the section taught by R.V. Cassill. I don't recall why I picked Verlin from the long list of available instructors. The catalog probably listed some publications. But everyone teaching there had equivalent lists. They were all real writers, certified by works in print.

On the first of weekly meetings, the classroom was crowded with about twenty students. Verlin, a small man with dark hair, thick eyebrows, and a sharp nose, sat behind a desk. He spoke softly and hesitantly in a deep voice, punctuating his words with hand gestures, immediately warning people that in his experience most people dropped the course early on, but that they could get a full refund if they made the decision that very night. No one left, though by the final weeks of the course only five of us showed up regularly.

At that point, after class Verlin and I regularly went to a bar across the street for a burger and a beer. He lamented of the stresses of making a living as a part-time writing teacher, forced to put aside his serious literary drafts to turn out quick potboiler novels for the paperback market of that time, frustrated by all the good ideas he was wasting to meet deadlines—characters and situations ripe for real delving had he the time. But one recent commentator on a Forgotten Books website who reread those works said, "Cassill seems to have used his pulp fiction to experiment with different techniques and subjects."

With life in New York not what he had hoped for, Verlin would be going back to Iowa, the state of his birth, where he had chopped off the tips of three fingers in a farming accident and later earned an MFA in the Writers' Workshop. He had taught there previously and would be teaching there again the following fall. The return to Iowa was good for him. He wrote a long novel, *Clem Anderson*, and after a few years moved on to Brown's creative writing faculty, where he wrote more fiction, helped found AWP (the Association of Writers and Writing Programs), compiled anthologies, and produced a text called *Fiction Writing* that's still available. His novels are as well, some digital and some used.

While I was in his New School class, Verlin didn't have much to say about the long-forgotten stories I was writing. He put them in a category with E.M. Forster's speculative fiction, a form he didn't get and didn't feel comfortable commenting on. Still, he encouraged me to apply to the Iowa Workshop, though I don't recall how enthusiastically. In any event, I was accepted, perhaps with a good word from him, perhaps a reward for listening to his woes.

Before Iowa, as I've explained, my knowing writers was rare. But you couldn't walk down the street in Iowa City without bumping into at least two or three, some pulling you aside to ask urgently if you were working on anything new. Of course, Workshop classrooms were packed with writers, spilling over into frequent parties held in cramped student housing and into booths with pitchers of watery 3.2 beer at a bar called Kenny's. Writers, writers everywhere and only swill to drink.

Even then, young as most of us were, we knew who

was destined for fame and awards, and the predictions were usually right, including likely laureates even before their was such a thing as a American poet laureate. Others, me included, developed more slowly, perhaps surprising themselves in the years ahead. Beyond the impetus to write and the collaborative revision advice, one of the important lessons of the Workshop was knowing that you weren't the only oddball in the crowd, the weirdo who skipped neighborhood small talk to put words on a clipboard.

After that—what with teaching colleagues, many students who achieve, and a longstanding fiction group—my life has overflowed with writer friends and acquaintances, or just writers with whom I've exchanged greetings, handshakes, and a few words of conversation. Because of who they are and whom they know, I estimate I'm two degrees of separation from most of the major writers of the Western world, as well as many in Africa and East Asia. Even if the great majority has no idea who I am, I consider myself very fortunate in these connections, the resonance of the panorama of the literary world. But that's just the surface. What lies beneath is another matter.

Where writers are concerned, the nature of knowing involves a degree of mystery. Non-writers have inner lives and secret thoughts, of course, but they don't express themselves on the page, revealing a very different depth and dimension than they express in normal conversation or even in moments of confessional revelation. Good writers reveal intricacies and insights in ways unavailable to them when they are being their social selves.

One friend, after reading a long essay that analyzed one of his best-known stories, told me, "I didn't know I was so smart." That is, the critic unearthed strategies and intricacies the writer had no idea existed. Did I do that? He did, but it wasn't a result of his conscious mind, instead the outcome of a process he couldn't really articulate. Perhaps my red-haired schoolmate had been drawn to profundities our teacher encoded within the words of the Wedge stories.

I learned very early on that the writer I know as a person, no matter how well, is not the writer whose words I read. Even when the material is autobiographical, even based on incidents I've heard about in great detail, the written version is another reality and the voice or character experiencing the situations a much more complex being than the person who told me about them. So, what does it actually mean to know a writer?

# *Roth's Complaint*

Philip Roth hated my short stories. I'd create them with a pen, transcribe the words to typescript with a manual Smith-Corona, and hand him a stack of paper, only to have them returned a week later with "Oh no!" "Too much!" and "Really?" scrawled in just about every margin. Never did he offer advice on how to improve them. Perhaps they were hopeless. One interminable story he didn't even finish. "I can't read any more."

Not that I blame him. They weren't very good, and they went on and on. In fact, not very good may be a euphemism for awful.  Once, as I walked to the front of the class, he put a thick manuscript of one story into my hand and asked, "Cummins, have you ever heard of the vignette?" Another time, when I attempted a sex scene, he announced, "Cummins, you can't handle breasts."

At the time, in the fall of 1960, Roth was twenty-seven and had just won the National Book Award for *Goodbye, Columbus*, and I was twenty-four in my first semester in the Iowa Writers' Workshop, wondering whether my admission had been a clerical error and whether I was deceiving myself as well as the committee. Roth was verifying my insecurities.

I had picked him as my initial workshop mentor because we shared a similar background, both of us New Jersey born and bred. Several college friends were from Newark, as well, and knew of him or had siblings who had gone to high school with him. A few even knew the affluent South Orange family he disparaged in his title novella.

Despite these seeming connections of place and age, we were worlds apart in talent and achievement, he already on his way to becoming a major American writer, me desperate to write a story he would deign to finish.

Actually, that semester he did like one of mine, even suggesting that I send it to an editor friend with his recommendation. That name-dropping resulted in a personalized rejection. But several years later that work became my first published story. Roth, at the time, offered one piece of advice, a visual gesture he suggested I have my main character make, demonstrating by pressing his open hands together and dropping his face into them, his chin resting on his thumbs. To this day, I can't find a way to put it into words.

Roth gave me a B for the semester, a grade I was happy to get away with. Rumor had it that he only gave three As, one to a clearly talented young man—John Yount—who went on to write a number of praised Southern novels, another to my freshman comp office mate—Richard Kim—whose novel *The Martyred* two years later became an international bestseller. (I once visited Kim at his Massachusetts home and was shown a glass-front bookcase filled with the many translations, the German with an analytical essay cellophane-wrapped to the hardcover.)

So Roth wasn't just picking on me. He never drove me to tears as he did others, devastated students coming away from conferences in a state of post-traumatic stress. A few tried being defensive. One reported, "But I told him I wasn't writing *Goodbye, Columbus*." It wasn't convincing.

Some of Roth's impatience with students like me may have resulted from his precocious success, publishing in major literary magazines, including *The New Yorker*, when still in his early twenties, while almost everyone else the same age was still floundering.

Students who felt destroyed after a class discussion of their work weren't victims of cruelty, I believe, but rather of Roth's exceptional comic sense. Jokes spilled from him. If he hadn't become a major American writer, he had the wit for a career as a major stand-up comedian. He couldn't *not* be funny. I recall a group of us sitting with him one afternoon in the student union, when someone asked him what his teaching title was. "My mother refers to me," he said "as, My son, the visiting lecturer.'" Another time he proposed that symbolism was invented by men who came out of World War II, got graduate degrees on the GI Bill, and found themselves teaching at colleges, with fifty minutes to fill three times a week. "So they came up with symbolism to have something to talk about."

When the next semester I was in a different fiction section that met on the other side of a narrow wall, we could hear Roth's class cracking up again and again. The time he led the group discussion of my story he liked, he spouted joke after joke, and I laughed along with everyone else because the story was, ultimately, a putdown of the main character, prime for spritzing. It was when he evoked laughter from someone's serious story—perhaps based on an autobiographical distress—that the student writer became distraught.

Roth was certainly civil to me as a person, no matter what he thought of my writings. On frigid days my VW bug wouldn't start, and I'd have to wrap up in a parka and walk through icy winds to cross the bridge over the Iowa River. Roth lived in a university-owned house on the west side of the river not far from my tin hut student housing.

Several times he stopped his long blue Lincoln to give me a ride to the main campus. Even though it was only a short trip, I did feel a certain formality about the occasion, the tall young man, elegant in tweeds, already exuding success, in full control over that big car.

I'll admit I wondered if I should take it personally when I read *Letting Go*, the novel that came out the next year, and encountered a nasty two-year-old named Walter. No. Probably just a coincidence.

Still, Roth obsessed many of my classmates. The great majority didn't know how to address him. No one I knew called him Philip. Mr. Roth felt odd because he wasn't much older than the rest of us. Yet his manner didn't invite intimacy. A friend, one of the people who got an A, told me of a nightmare about Roth somehow looking like Emiliano Zapata, mustache and all, and awakening in fright. Another friend was bird watching one afternoon and saw Roth approach with a group of people. "I just ran in panic," he reported.

I recall one night during a workshop party at Vance Bourjaily's house in the village of West Branch, birthplace of Herbert Hoover, when one student notorious for nightly drunkenness and fathering children walked (staggered?) up to Roth and his then-wife Maggie and announced, "I don't know what to call you. I don't think you're the kind of guy I could invite to dinner." "Try me," Roth said. The invitation was offered. I wonder what that dinner would have been like, Roth coping with a swarm of toddlers, several in diapers, his nervous host in his cups. Roth no doubt made the adults laugh as he took mental notes for a chaotic domestic scene that might appear in some future novel.

Speaking of Maggie, we were so wrong about that

relationship. I recall people thinking, in the context of so many troubled faculty and student marriages, that at least the Roths had a good one. That was before news of the disastrous separation and Roth's apparent churning out of stories to find money for support. One woman student even claimed he stole a plot idea from her. In the recent PBS American Masters profile, more than fifty years later, "Philip Roth: Unmasked," Roth said of the crash of his first marriage that it traumatized him and paralyzed his ability to write. The program ignores his second marriage to the British actress Claire Bloom and the devastating post-divorce book she wrote about him. Wives, it appears, were not for him.

The American Masters treatment came out on the occasion of Roth's eightieth birthday. Even in the latest photos he looks good, walking with vigorous strides despite the history of debilitating back pain he claims made him contemplate suicide. In the interviews he reveals an apparent obsession with death, the subject of several of his recent books. But, although I've seen photos of him as he has aged over many years, it was those taken around the time of our Iowa years that connected most with me.

Over the decades, I've dined out—literally—on having been Philip Roth's student. One evening in a private room in a Manhattan restaurant among of group of people who enjoyed great success in law and medicine, a friend mentioned the fact. It was as if a nimbus suddenly glowed over my head. The importance of the others diminished at once, all eager to know what it was like.

A more specific question from writers has been what did I learn from Roth. Of course, there were the jokes, the repeated one-liners that still get laughs. But I really didn't learn much about writing, nothing I couldn't have gained from a close reading of his early stories. The actual lessons from that semester were much less about writing than about how to be a writer, specifically how to become inured to rejection and even mockery. It was like the lesson of falling off a bicycle and getting back on right away, training wheels gone. Even if he hadn't praised one of my stories, I don't think I would have stopped trying.

Tales about Roth in more recent years have him discouraging people from writing, exhorting them to avoid a life of creative anguish, as well as announcing how relieved he feels after retiring as a writer at age eighty, the awful weight lifted from his shoulders. Even at the start of his career he may have been rehearsing that shtick on some students. As far as I know, it didn't take for any of us. He certainly wrote on and on, book after book, regardless of how much it made him suffer.

It's been a half century, and the memories remain vivid. I still wouldn't know how to address him if I ever met him again. I don't know if he'd accept an invitation to dinner. I certainly wouldn't want him to see this piece and return it with one marginal exclamation after another.

# Knowing Vance Bourjaily

When I turned to the *New York Times* obituary page on September 3, 2010 and saw Vance Bourjaily's name spread across the top, I surprised myself with the sudden clutch of sadness. Perhaps it was the accompanying photo, Vance in 1960, the year I first met him, a man only in his late thirties. Perhaps I was mourning my own past as much as Vance's death, the sudden reminiscence of his role in it.

The last time I had seen him was in 1965, though I had read several of his novels after that—*The Man Who Knew Kennedy, The Fake Book,* etc.—and had a brief letter grom him in the 1980s when I was editing *The Literary Review* and published an interview with him. He thanked me and said something nice about the magazine. I was a bit surprised that he remembered me. All those years and all those students. But Vance was a kind man in person and must have been as generous in his memories.

The *Times* obituary was a long one. He had to be important to receive so much space. Though the high points of his literary career had come decades ago, and even though he never became the major novelist many had expected him to be in those days, the *Times* authenticated his legacy, noting that "he figured prominently when critics made lists of writers who were underappreciated or whose promise had gone unfulfilled. But he had a long and substantial career in letters of the sort that was far more prevalent a half-century ago than it is today." By implication, his role in American writing was more significant than his now forgotten works.

It wasn't until recently that I read a reissue of Dan Wakefield's *New York in the Fifties* and learned of Vance's role in the post-war New York literary scene. Already known for his 1947 postwar novel, *The End of My* Life, published when he was 25, Vance functioned as a sort of social chairman, organizing gatherings of writers like Norman Mailer, Calder Willingham, John W. Aldrich, John Clellon Holmes (who later taught at Iowa), and others on Sundays at the White Horse Tavern, according to Mailer "twenty times or more." He also edited the magazine *Discovery* that published the work of many writers who went on to significant careers.

His many books are available on Amazon, but none in new editions, all used. It's an unhappy reality for all but a miniscule fraction of writers that despite good reviews and the attention of critics, most books are forgotten along with the names of their authors. That small period of fame is the most any writer can hope for, and few achieve even that. Vance had his. How do the novels hold up? I have several on a bookshelf and should reread them.

It's likely the one incident that bonded us, and made him remember who I was, resulted from my listening to the radio one afternoon in the summer of 1961. At the time I was in New York back from Iowa City and living in a sublet, roach-ridden, fifth-floor walkup on St. Marks Place. Hemingway had days before put a shotgun in his mouth and blown his brains out, some said because he was obsessed about becoming an unknown, his books ultimately obscure. Leslie Fiedler was talking about Hemingway on WBAI as I puttered around the apartment, but I focused my attention when he noted that Hemingway considered Vance the best American writer under 40. Back in Iowa City in late August, assuming that he was aware of the praise, I congratulated Vance and learned that the Hemingway stamp of approval was news to him. Immediately, he called his agent. Apparently, it was a big deal, and I the bearer of good tidings.

Fiedler had added he disagreed with Hemingway, but that didn't matter.

I wouldn't have called Vance a personal friend, not in the sense of his relationship with some other MFA students who were his hunting, fishing, and drinking buddies. But he was open and accessible. While certain other faculty members were Mister until you developed a first name connection equivalent to the French shift from *vous* to *tu*, he was immediately, "Call me Vance."

He played softball with us on Saturday mornings, hosted occasional parties on Saturday nights. My greatest moment in sports—especially because I'm uncoordinated and spent a boyhood of ineptitude on playing fields—came when Vance was pitching and I drove a triple deep into right field, putting good wood to the underhand toss of an almost-major American novelist.

He threw a few parties for the entire writers' workshop, students and faculty, at least that I attended, but they were memorable, taking place in his house a few miles from Iowa City in the tiny town of West Branch, birthplace of Herbert Hoover, Vance repeating his hosting of the White Horse days. Was there live jazz? Certainly music of some source, and food and drink, and eager conversation, the rooms packed, *Gemütlichkeit* abounding. I've been told that in recent years MFA students and faculty rarely mix, off in distinct social realms. I hope that's not accurate. So much of the workshop experience came from that informal interaction, which may have been more valuable than the actual instruction.

Vance and other instructors used their connections to connect students with editors. For a year or so he had a first reading contract with *The New Yorker*, which meant that the magazine paid him a fixed sum for the right of first refusal of whatever he wrote. That may have been about the time *The Violated* was published. I recall him sending his editor a story by one of the best student writers, a man who went on to publish a number of novels. The story wasn't taken but did elicit a note of praise. At that stage of a student's career a good word from *The New Yorker* was equivalent to a Hemingway encomium.

I don't recall any Bourjaily parties after the death of his daughter, Anna, at age twelve, an appealing young girl who mingled with the happy crowd. It was an accident, Vance driving a yellow roofless Volkswagen vehicle on a country road before the days of seatbelts, Anna and a friend, the daughter of a psychology professor, in the back seat. For some reason the car had to swerve, and both girls were thrown out and killed. That was 1964 when I was the father of two daughters, one a toddler and one an infant, unable to fathom how I would cope with such a loss. The memorial service in the university chapel was just chamber music, deep and mournful. No one spoke. I shook Vance's hand outside on the lawn and felt helpless. He thanked me for coming.

His marriage to Tina lasted until the mid eighties, after he left Iowa to teach at the University of Arizona for 1980 to 1985. Then he moved on to Louisiana State as director of the creative writing program until he retired in the late nineties. Vance was 87 and living in California with his second wife, Yasmin Mogul, when he died from a brain hemorrhage after a fall.

The image of Vance I carry with me most is the man, not very tall, stocky, dressed in a wool plaid shirt and heavy outdoors trousers at the front on the room in a metal war surplus classroom along the Iowa River, leaning back on a chair, his thick hunting books propped on a wooden table as he taught.

What he actually said in the classroom is lost on me. But he was the source of one piece of distinct writing instruction I still retain after all these years. In the fifties while living in New York he wrote many half-hour television scripts and was told by the old hands that when bringing a new character into a story be sure to have the existing characters express an opinion about him or her so that the audience is prepared with expectation. I've shared that wisdom with several generations of students.

As much as he was a writer, Vance was an outdoorsman, collaborating with his son Philip, himself an outdoors writer, on many books and articles for magazines like *Field and Stream*. One day I was checking out books at the Iowa university library, when Vance came in with a request for the one book he insisted no library should be without. I lingered, eager for the advice of a master. It turned out to be a work about fly-fishing.

Certainly hunting was more important to Vance than the faculty conference about my PhD dissertation. In those days, you could follow up the MFA at Iowa with a PhD, fulfilling the same course, examination, and orals requirements as the scholars but substituting a creative work for the dissertation. I suppose that once he approved my novel

Vance didn't see the necessity of showing up with the rest of the committee for a pro forma hour. The group had to have a representative of another discipline, an economist on mine who asked me what the novel has to say about the economic side of human existence. I made up an answer and forget what anyone else asked, but when it was over Robert Scholes, later famous for his role in structuralism and semiotics, called me aside and said, "You don't want to publish that novel," implying that it would harm whatever career I might have. Fortunately, agents and publishers complied and saved me that embarrassment. By the way, a number of Scholes' books are still available on Amazon, both new and in Kindle versions.

I never blamed Vance for not showing up. Even at the time I found it amusing. After all, I was past that novel and on to another. I didn't want to be bothered with that session either. Besides, I felt a debt to Vance. He did give me some advice about the dissertation novel, enough to make it acceptable. That work, deficient as it was, got me a PhD, a teaching job, eventually tenure and publication of stories and some books, though nothing to excite a Hemingway or a Fiedler. Maybe Vance saw beyond that first novel; maybe he just took a flyer on me. But primarily I owe him for being an affirmative presence, a good guy, a writer who cared about other writers, including uncoordinated fledglings with a long way to go.

# Gaytys and Dangs: Echoing George P. Elliott

*When the magazine* da Cunha *accepted my story "Among the Gaytys," the editors asked for a blog about its origin. My story is an overt knockoff—most obvious in its title—of George P. Elliott's once well-known story, one I wanted to revisit for years, about a young anthropologist dropped into the village of a strange remote people. But George also set an example for reinventing the stories of others, including Henry James' "The Aspern Papers" and Swift's "A Modest Proposal." I consider myself in good company.*

My story title, "Among the Gaytys," is a deliberate emulation of George P. Elliott's "Among the Dangs" and a homage to a man who was my mentor long ago at the Iowa Writers' Workshop. For many in a certain writers' generation the connection would be an automatic reflex: hear George's name and "Among the Dangs" would pop into your mind. It's his most famous story and the title of his once best-known collection, a book filled with stories that had been recognized with O. Henry and similar awards. "Dangs" itself was first published in *Esquire* in 1958. But now, sadly, George has been dead for many years and his literary reputation diminished to an obscure footnote.

Beyond the title echo, I deliberately didn't reread "Dangs" in my autographed copy of the collection till after I wrote my own story. It turns out that what we have in common is a young anthropologist working on a degree sent to live among a primitive people to collect data for a thesis. But George told his story in the first person and covered a number of visits to the South American jungle world of the Dangs over several decades, including a "marriage" to a Dang woman and a half Dang son. George's character takes on a role as an important seer in the Dang community. My Dwight is never anything but a shunned outsider, with the Gaytys only once for a single year.

George told a group of us his Dang origin tale. He had been accepted into the artists' community of Yaddo but felt trapped by the rules of the place, what he considered a form of confinement. He couldn't bear to stay there the full term of the residency, and the night before he was about to pack up and leave, he endured a disturbing dream that contained the basics of "Among the Dangs." It doesn't take a psychologist to realize the displaced and trapped thematic connections between George at Yaddo and his fictional anthropologist in the Dang village. Interestingly, although George knew very little about anthropology, his creative imagination convinced a number of professionals that he was an expert. Some dream.

Rather than through a dream in the midst of confinement, my source for the Gaytys was an anecdote friends told me about their son's residence in a remote Russian village among an isolated native people. At that time, the son was a PhD student writing a dissertation; now he's a faculty member. The Russian government's official assumption about those native people had them wearing colorful garb in their daily lives. But during the time my friends' son lived among them, they wore ordinary clothing until a delegation of Russian authorities was scheduled to visit. Then they pulled out what amounted to their costumes and no doubt amused themselves by putting one over on officialdom.

There was, I knew, a short story in that material. Garb would be involved. But when I sat down to actually write, what came out was not at all what I expected, no authorities to be tricked, no young anthropologist in on the joke. The Gaytys don't clown around. They have no sense of humor, at least not any that Dwight can discern in a full year. But what are they up to?

George ends "Among the Dangs" with a profound moral conundrum, typical of his work. His narrator has contributed to knowledge, received tenure and a professorship, thereby pleasing his American wife, but he wonders: "... whereas if I had stayed there among the Dangs much longer I would have reverted until I had become one of them, might not have minded when the time came to die under the sacrificial knife, would have taken in all ways the risk of prophecy—as my Dang son intended to do—until I had lost myself utterly."

My own writerly inclination is more existential than moral, and the ambiguity of my ending disturbs some readers. Dwight just walks off. What happens to his seeming fried Gryx? Who or what is lost? Those frustrated readers demand to know. Perhaps the answer will come to me in a dream some night.

# Richard E. Kim's
# The Martyred: *Fleeting Fame*

When I read that the novelist Susan Choi, in her quest for her Korean literary roots, had never heard of Richard E. Kim or his 1964 novel, *The Martyred*, I was dumbstruck. The man and his book have had an ongoing presence in my memories for decades. I was there at the beginning, while it was being written, then a witness to the phenomenal success of the novel throughout the world. Choi, daughter of a Korean father, notes in her foreword to the 2011 Penguin Classics republication of *The Martyred* that "Richard K. Kim had never been discussed at the Asian American reading group, he had never appeared on the syllabus." Even after an older Korean man gave her a copy, the novel sat unopened on her bookshelves for another decade.

Fame is fleeting, and obscurity looms. But still, not even to know of Kim's existence. After all, how many Korean writers have ever enjoyed such international recognition and prominence?

When I visited Kim (that's how we addressed him, never Richard) at his home in Shutesbury, Massachusetts, in 1968, he showed me a three-tier, glass-front bookcase filled with editions in many languages. I was struck—and he was amused—by the German translation with an analytical pamphlet wrapped to the book with cellophane.

No one expected the novel to take off the way it did. The publisher, George Braziller, normally an outlet for art books and some important poets, never before had experienced a bestseller, scrambling to outsource printing as U.S. sales reached 60,000 hard-cover copies. The rush began with a laudatory full-page review in the *St. Louis Post Dispatch* and was followed by many more, including Chad Walsh's front-page review in *The New York Times Book Review* of February 16, 1964, in which he said:

> ...his purpose here is not to tell the deeds of war but to probe the involutions and ambiguities of conscience—the meaning of suffering and of evil and holiness, the uncertain boundaries between illusion and truth. This he has done with a skill so great it is almost invisible.

*Life* magazine, one of this country's most successful weeklies in the mid 1960s, published a photo feature called "Best-Selling Korean" with Kim; his wife, Penny, on a backyard swing; and their two children, David and Melissa, sitting on their father's lap. It was rare then as it is now for a new writer to take up pages in a magazine with a circulation of more than eight million.

I met Kim in Iowa City fifty-five years ago, in 1960. He was my officemate in a converted army barrack that housed the freshman writing graduate assistants. Before I actually saw him in person, I had heard much about him and viewed his photograph—stern-faced and seemingly foreboding. Just in his late twenties, he already had been an officer in the South Korean Army during the Korean War, a general's aide, and eventually one of the two Koreans to serve on the UN Truce Team. He came to Iowa with an MA from the Johns Hopkins' writing program. I was less than a novice, still bewildered that they had let me into the program, half expecting to be revealed as a clerical error.

He—the idea of him—intimidated me before I even met him.

And yet we became good friends, to the point where I stood with him when he applied for his American citizenship, drove him to an army-navy surplus store in Cedar Rapids for our winter coats, and brought Penny and their first child, David, home from the university hospital. Those were pre-Pampers days, when all diapers were cloth and delivered by a service. I remember Kim pacing around their living room, constantly reaching into the crib to check the newborn's diaper, and changing at the slightest dampness, despite Penny's urgings to relax. Hardly a stern, foreboding man.

With his MFA he got a position teaching in the MFA program at the University of Massachusetts in Amherst, where I visited twice and saw him in New York several times to receive copies of his two books after *The Martyred*. He moved to teach at Long Beach State and San Diego State, and we lost touch, mainly because of my own personal dilemmas. I still regret that very much. If that had been a time of email and cell phones, I'm sure we would have stayed in contact.

But back to Susan Choi and her ignorance of his name. It's not just that he wrote a well-reviewed novel. What happened was more like what's said about Lord Byron—he woke up one morning and found himself famous.

*The Martyred* stayed on *The New York Times* bestseller list for twenty weeks, selling more than 1,000 copies a day in March 1964. It was translated into ten different languages, and made into a play, an opera, and a film. Pearl S. Buck, herself a Nobel Prize winner, predicted, "If this young man continues to do so well as this, he will someday be worthy of the Nobel Prize."

And Kim was nominated for the prize in the early 1980s. By that time *The Martyred* had received a previous nomination for the National Book Award and Kim, a Guggenheim grant and a National Endowment for the Arts Literary Fellowship.

His next novel, *The Innocent,* in 1968, after a big—for the time—advance from Houghton Mifflin, received mediocre reviews as it continued the story of the first novel's narrator, Captain Lee, now a major. That novel is twice as long as *The Martyred.* I remember how nervous Kim was about it and his worries about its reception. It's very different to be a suddenly discovered unknown than to be a writer with a good part of the literary world looking over your shoulder as you type. At least that's how it was in Kim's mind, and he was not wrong, at least in his anxiety over being judged by the standard of his first book.

Here's Kim on being a writer in America in a 1993 interview:

> When *The Martyred* attracted all that attention, I learned about the writing game in this country—about agents, publicists, public relations, people, talk shows. It was flattering and seductive, but it was also scary and unpleasant.

I remember his anxiety back in Iowa City when his was about to be interviewed for a Korean broadcast of the *Voice of America.* Hours before the phone call he told me he was blanking and feared he had forgotten his native language. Of course, he hadn't.

Heinz Insu Fenkl, in his introduction to the Penguin Classic edition of *The Martyred,* attributes timing to the tepid reception of *The Innocent* when it was released. The anti-war sentiment during the Vietnam War, he says, made many critics and readers uncomfortable and negative.

Kim supported that war because of his antipathy to Communism from his Korean War experience, including a pre-war childhood in the North. During a meal in a New York Korean restaurant he told me he thought it necessary to stop the spread of Communism, perhaps conflating the North Vietnamese with the North Koreans. He also warned me that the food was very spicy.

Ironically, anti-war protesters burned down the freshman comp building that housed the Iowa office we shared. If it matters to anyone, I was opposed to the war from the beginning, marched and carried signs, though Kim and I never argued about it.

*The Innocent* hasn't been reprinted. But Kim's third book, *Lost Names: Scenes from a Korean Boyhood,* does have a 2011 edition from The University of California Press. Fenkl calls the work "a collection of loosely autobiographic stories," and others refer to it as that. But Kim told me it was essentially about the facts of his early life. Of course, the first publication came years before the popularity of memoirs, when all stories, no matter how close to real events, were considered fiction.

The title story, "Lost Names," tells of a time during Kim's youth in North Korea when the Japanese conquerors of all Korea forced the natives to climb to a Shinto temple to receive Japanese names that replaced their real Korean names.

Kim is quoted as saying he had no animosity toward the Japanese. But I remember an embarrassed confession he made to me. Penny, not yet his wife, was taking courses at NYU, and he waited in a hallway outside a classroom for her. A young Japanese man, recognizing Kim as a fellow

Asian, came up to him to chat. Kim lost it, ranting at the man and chasing him away. As he recounted what he did, he admitted his shame.

In *Lost Names,* Kim writes of his father, who was a national hero in Korea for his resistance to the Japanese occupation and to the North Koreans. Despite the father's reputation, because of forced retirement rules in South Korea at the time, he became a man without a role at a relatively young age. In that, ironically, he may have prefigured his son's becoming forgotten.

Kim never wrote another work of fiction after *Lost Names* in 1971. He did maintain a career in the literary world—translating, representing Korean authors, compiling photo books, writing Korean newspaper columns and a children's book, and helping produce and narrate documentaries in Korea. Over the years I received rumors that he was back in Korea, which he was for a time. But I'm not sure how he divided his residences. But his obituary reports that he died in Shutesbury in 2009 with his family around him. His obituary noted memorial donations should be sent to a hospice. In the years I knew him he was a heavy smoker. Sad as I am that I let the friendship fade, I'm sadder that he gave up writing.

One detail I share with Susan Choi is a copy of *The Martyred* on my bookshelves. But mine was autographed on 12/25/63, and I read it immediately. I don't know if Kim's choice of Christmas day was deliberate, but it is ironic timing for the novel in which Christian belief lies at the core of the story and the characters' torments.

The novel is part mystery and part existential conundrum. The narrator, Captain Lee, an intelligence officer, is given the assignment of establishing what actually happened when the North Korean communists shot twelve Christian ministers. His superior, Colonel Chang, hopes to turn the event into useful propaganda by establishing that the murdered ministers were martyrs. Captain Lee first must interrogate two surviving ministers, Mr. Shin and Mr. Hann. Chang wishes to prove they lived because they betrayed those killed. What actually happened is much more tangled, Lee's investigation complicated by Mr. Shin's initial silence and several reversals in his later explanations. Complex questions of faith and belief emerge, and what had started as a search for specific information becomes an existential quest into the essence of human existence in a tragic world.

While the question of who betrayed the ministers dominates the story, less space is devoted to a perhaps even greater act of betrayal. The Chinese communists have entered the war, and the overwhelmed South Korean army is about to abandon the already bombed out city of Pyongyang. Captain Lee describes the view from his office window in the early pages of the novel: "From the white-blue November sky of North Korea, a cold gust swept down the debris-ridden slope, whipping up here and there dazzling snow flurries, smashing against the ugly, bullet-riddled buildings of Pyongyang." The army deliberately fails to warn the population that an even greater destruction is about to descend.

War seems to be an impetus for such works of literature. Kim dedicated *The Martyred* to Albert Camus and quotes him for an epigraph. Camus' writings sustained him through the Korean war.

*The Martyred* shares much with *The Plague*. Camus' characters, though memorable in themselves, are more representative of various beliefs and approaches to the crises of this world. Kim's characters also reveal ways of behaving and relating to the extremes of war, suffering, and death. How should we behave? What should we do when faced with a moral dilemma? What should we believe? What must we do to sustain ourselves and others?

Fenkl, in his introduction, reports that Kim had been disappointed by 20th-century American literature for failing to be "the voice and the conscience of the people."

That revelation explained to me why Kim asked the same question every time the Iowa fiction sections gathered for a joint session. We'd all talk about a work for an hour or two, but near the end of the period, Kim, sitting in the back of the room, would raise his hand and ask in the guise of an inscrutable Oriental, "Is this story?" He never dropped his articles in conversation. Why then? It was mysterious and befuddling.

I understand now that Kim had a different conception of what a story should be than the rest of the people in that room. He wasn't interested in human interaction as such, but rather what people did or should do at times of existential crisis. For Kim, his fictional imagination was inseparable from his deepest concerns. Addressing them, he believed, is what fiction should do.

In many ways the first half of The Martyred resembles a traditional mystery novel, with variations of familiar plot and character matters, and as in all mysteries essential explanations are contained in backstory that the seekers must unearth. It's almost exactly in the middle—after the revelations of the captured North Korean explain what actually happened with the ministers—that the novel turns from more conventional mystery detection to existential mysteries and unknowns. That's not to say, the second half doesn't offer several crucial surprise revelations; but none of the other characters were seeking or expecting them.

One commentary sums it up:

> With strong existentialist themes, the story deals with issues of human suffering, the meanings of truth, the human conscience, and the nature of good and evil. The novel addresses larger questions about Christianity itself as well, exploring issues of faith, hope, confession, martyrdom, and betrayal.

Referring to Christian mysteries, Captain Lee notes: "I'm not much for mysteries." At bit later, "I have no use for fairy tales." He sympathizes with the suffering and despair of the Christians, but he does not love them. The question of fairy tales lies at the heart of belief and responsibility.

Colonel Chang, needing twelve martyrs for propaganda purposes, cares nothing for religion. "If there really is a god who can observe from high up in heaven what we down here are doing," he says, "it surely must look rather childish."

But the novel reveals that doubt is widespread. Ultimately, Mr. Shin—who sacrifices himself by lying about what happened to the murdered ministers to protect their memory—reveals that he does not believe: "I found only man with his sufferings...and death, inexorable death!" Mr. Shin finally urges: "Bear your cross with courage, courage to fight despair, to love man, to have pity on mortal man."

When asked if he despises the Christians, Captain Lee answers that it's the deception that bothers him, the Christians being lied to. "And meanwhile the people continue to suffer, continue to die, deceived from birth to death."

At the end, Lee receives conflicting reports of Mr. Shin's fate—that he is dead, that he is being seen all over the North, as if resurrected. He serves as the doubter who provides meaning and comfort to so many.

I'm reminded of the ending of Joseph Conrad's *Heart of Darkness*, where Marlow, the narrator, haunted by his memory of Mr. Kurtz's last words—"The Horror! The Horror!"—will not tell Mr. Kurtz's intended the truth of what happened to her fiancé, as much as he hates a lie. He allows her to exist in her delusion, for to do otherwise would destroy her. Was Kim influenced? I know that he admired Conrad and identified with him as an author who also wrote in a third language.

On the closing pages Captain Lee joins the refugees in a national song "with a wondrous lightness of heart hitherto unknown to me." Note that it is not a hymn. But he has accepted the others as "my people" and experiences a human connection.

At the conclusion of his *Times* review, Chad Walsh speculates on the ambiguity of the novel's ending:

> Perhaps the novel is saying that mankind can live only by illusion, and that the saint is the unbeliever who preaches illusion, at whatever inner cost to his own rational integrity. Or perhaps it implies that the apparent illusion proclaimed out of love for mankind is not illusion at all; that indeed it is the only real thing in a world that is otherwise meaningless flux, horror, and chaos.

He concludes the *The Martyred* is "a magnificent achievement, and it will last."

We should remind ourselves that we have experienced

the novel in a country where we enjoy relative safety, able to focus on our personal fulfillment and happiness. But we have only to read a newspaper or watch TV news to realize how many millions exist amid flux, horror, and chaos. It's the fear that lurks in our nightmares.

While rereading I was often moved by revisiting a story I already knew. Walsh is right that the novel is an achievement, but—unfortunately—he was wrong that it would last. May it be rediscovered and reborn.

**Notes:**
Additional information about Richard E. Kim is available at these sites:

- www.richardekim.com
- "Another War Raged Within," a review by Chad Walsh in *The New York Times* (16 February 1964)
- "Best-selling Korean: Kim writes a remarkable novel," an article in the "Books" section of *Life* magazine (20 March 1964, pages 125-126); includes photographs of Kim, his wife Penelope, and his children David and Melissa as toddlers

# *Iowa Writers in the Sixties*

*One afternoon after planning the sequence of pieces in this collection, I had the idea of listing all the writers I knew at Iowa, in addition to the Workshop faculty members and one fellow student I've already written about. To my surprise, I came up with about twenty-five names, surely forgetting some and not including those I didn't know or remember well enough to say anything about in the vignettes that follow. These memories are much more anecdotal than literary, though I've read the novels, stories, and poems of many. Web searches after the compilation of the list revealed that some had died in recent months, in addition to the deaths I already knew about. Given the ages of my contemporaries, that's no surprise. But in my mind, when I think about them, I see young faces, promises yet to be fulfilled, though most were, perhaps not to the hoped-for stature of their dreams. Still, not everyone can be a major writer. The world doesn't have room for so many. Back then what drove us was just to be published, and it happened sooner or later. Given the scheme of things, that should count as success, although many in this group went on to real fame, if not fortune.*

*What follows is random, the order in which the names popped into my memory. My memory is also to blame for any errors or confusions and may differ from those of others who were there at the same time and in the same places. After all, it was a long time ago.*

## William Cotter Murray

Bill was born in County Clare, emigrating while very young, still speaking with a bit of a brogue. For a few years, we shared an office for the technical writing faculty in the College of Engineering building. I didn't spend time with him away from that office, but found his Irish charm appealing. What does stick with me was how thin his legs were, though I never actually saw them not covered by the wide flapping trousers he wore. When he crossed those legs, there seemed to be no substance under the cloth as if he were a stick figure. That perception may have been mine alone; I never mentioned it to anyone else.

Bill did, when still in that office, publish a novel called *Michael Joe*, which won the Meredith award and was broadcast as a radio play across Ireland. I still have a signed copy, a kind note that he someday hoped to read something of mine. Beyond the award, the novel won him a position on the Iowa faculty that he held until his retirement.

I rediscovered Bill in the 2002 documentary *Stone Reader*, about Mark Moskowitz's—the filmmaker's—search for a writer from Iowa named Dow Mossman, who had published a 552-page novel titled *The Stones of Summer* and who was called a "superior talent" in *The New York Times*' review. Moskowitz came upon the work in a used bookshop and felt compelled to track down the author, who seemingly had disappeared for thirty years.

The tangled mysteries of Moskowitz's quest are a bit of a red herring because he knew early on that Bill had been Mossman's Workshop mentor but delayed reaching out to him till other clues failed. But Bill knew exactly where Mossman could be found, debilitated by a writer's block, working in a Cedar Rapids metal shop. If Moskowitz had called Bill at the start, the mystery would have been solved immediately. Of course, he wouldn't have had a movie.

And there was Bill on the screen, white-haired and retired, still thin and still with a face and accent I remembered. He reveals, "I remember he [Mossman] was pretty strung out, and a couple of times he just had to stop to save his sanity. Being a mentor on that book was one of the toughest assignments I ever had." Bill died in 2016 in Iowa City, having left behind several children. I believe I had heard about the birth of the first, now a person of late middle age.

### Clark Blaise and Bharati Mukherjee

It's impossible for me of think of them separately because, with the exception of a few months, they were a couple soon after they met in Iowa City, she an MA, graduate of a college in India, a Brahman, attractive and exotic in a sari, he the son of a troubled marriage between a French Canadian father and an English Canadian mother that became the subject of much of his writing. Marrying Clark caused a bit of a scandal for Bharati given the expectation of her caste and her family. They collaborated on a book about their mixed cultural relationship, *Days and Nights in Calcutta*. But, ironically, as much as they are linked in my memory, they spent much of their marriage apart with teaching positions in different areas of the country, together for summer programs and at several points in their lives sharing a single faculty position.

Clark was one of those already touted when he arrived in the Workshop, known for the imprimatur of Bernard Malamud after a summer writing session at Harvard. The two—student and mentor—remained close, Clark naming his and Bharati's second son Bernard. Clark's many books have proved Malamud prescient.

Although getting her MFA, Bharati focused on a PhD in comparative literature, writing a dissertation on the Indian influences in the novels of Herman Hesse. But a story published in *The Atlantic* got the attention of Houghton Mifflin, which encouraged a novel, the first of many, and also story collections that led to her long faculty career at Berkeley and a reputation as a significant American writer.

I heard from them twenty years after our Iowa time when they needed teaching positions, having given up joint tenure at Skidmore. Clark, optimistically, thought he could earn a living as an author after a large for the time advance for a novel called *Lusts*. Bharati had an offer to teach world literature at Montclair State University. When she heard the teaching load was twelve credits, she thought that was for the year, not the semester it actually was.

The three of us met for dinner at a restaurant in the town of Montclair, where we discussed an issue of *The Literary Review*, which I was editing at the time, to be called "The Indian Commonwealth." Bharati, the guest editor, gathered works from well-known Indian diaspora authors from around the world and included her own story "The Middleman." It became the title story of a collection that won the National Book Critics Award for Fiction in a year, for some reason, there was no National Book Award. The recognition led to a position at Queens College with less of a teaching load and, a couple of years later, the big time at Berkeley.

Clark had the idea for an issue devoted to Canadian short stories and a friend, John Metcalf, who would edit it. The issue contained a reprint of one of Clark's stories, along with a detailed analysis to be included in a book about Clark's oeuvre. That was before email, and I sent Clark a photocopy of the essay, which led him to say, "I didn't know I was that smart," and gave me evidence to support the authorial fallacy, the mistaken assumption that authors really know what their works are about, as if the writing was fulfillment of a rational plan rather than imaginative instinct.

Although I have been in touch with Clark by email on occasion since the mid 1980s, the last time I actually saw him was when he visited Alison, my long-term present wife, and me with his son Bart, captivating us with his endless supply of anecdotes and his captivating ability as a raconteur.

I learned of Bharati's serious illness when a mutual friend wrote her to request a blurb for his story collection and she wrote back that she was too sick to do it. Although news of her death saddened me, it wasn't a surprise, but not the information in an obituary that Bart had died a number of years before from a hereditary disease carried by a gene from Clark's side of the family. Clark has written a forthcoming book about his love for his son and his great grief, *The Cruelest Gift: Inherited Disease in the Age of DNA*. This work joins Clark's twenty or so other books.

I prefer to remember the elegant woman and the exceptionally clever young man whose company was such a treat when we were young.

### Tom Kakonis

I had lost track of Tom for years from the time I moved back to New Jersey, wondering what ever happened to him after Iowa. We both hung around for several years post

MFA to get a PhD. Had he become an academic rather than a writer? Then I came upon an April 1980 news item about a student named Thomas Kakonis shooting and killing an accounting professor who had failed him at the Michigan college where his father was an assistant dean. After being arrested the young man was in a "near catatonic state." I probably had seen him as a child, though there were so many kids in Iowa City back then, mine included, that it was impossible to keep them all straight. I did feel a rush of compassion for Tom, trying to imagine how he could possibly cope.

But in the years since, as a search revealed, he had become a writer of crime novels, called heir-apparent to Elmore Leonard in blurbs. One series is about "Tim Waverly – a loveable gambler who constantly finds himself playing a game of survival against the odds." He also wrote darker thrillers under the pseudonym Adam Barrow. One called *Flawless* was picked as a People Magazine Chiller of the Week. In an online interview, Tom reveals that he didn't publish his first novel until he was 57 and that he learned much about the life of crime teaching inmates at Joliet prison in Illinois.

Back when we were in our twenties we had desks in that technical writing faculty office, where William Cotter Murray occupied a small private cubical. Tom had, like me, some experience in real technical writing and real service in the army, while I was only a six-monther. I recall him a lean and muscular, tense and intense.

We were founding members, as were all our officemates, of the Technical Writing Athletic Society, a diversion created to ease our minds from the pressures of writing and graduate course work. We would entertain ourselves and escape by bowling, shooting pool, and such. It's probably no surprise that our sporting hobby became more competitive than our academic and creative lives, each of us deadly eager to show up the others with our skills. Back in the office, people couldn't tear themselves away from the compulsion of pitching pennies against a wall to see whose could come closest. Engineering students would appear for conferences about their papers and find their instructors so immersed in the penny game that they had to wait to be recognized.

Perhaps my strongest memory of Tom in our Iowa days is the very public affair he had with the poet wife of a young assistant professor in the English Department. They made no effort to be private or discreet. One night a group of us, Tom's wife Sharon included, were sitting in a booth in Kenny's tavern when Tom and Mary walked in, the rest of us much more nonplussed than they were, exchanging frenetic whispers and avoiding eye contact with Sharon. Mary probably glared. She was a severe woman, a visual mismatch for her soft, meek husband. Sharon, with her coiffed dark hair and painted nails, looked as if she had been varnished.

Sharon must have kicked Tom out of their house because I have a vague memory of him sleeping on a couch in the home of another mutual friend. Long ago I wrote a story based on the situation, though now I couldn't tell you what was taken from actuality and what I made up. Back then I heard a rumor that he and Sharon got together again. When I recently checked White Pages, I saw another woman's name at his address, apparently a different wife, though for how long I have no idea. Apparently, he's had the most dramatic life of us all. I wonder whatever happened to his son.

**Andrew Fetler**

I've known many obsessive writers but none more so than Andy. It was a toss up whether he'd show at a Saturday night party when everyone else was very much in the mood for a break. Most of the time his then-wife, Carol, would call to report that they couldn't make it because Andy was in the midst of a creative burst. (Carol, by the way, was widely considered a lookalike for Mary Travers of Peter, Paul, and Mary.)

All those hours devoted to writing didn't get into the way of Andy's social activism and outrage. During a period of civil rights tension, he wrote a letter to the *Press-Citizen* in the voice of a bigoted landlord refusing to rent to people of color. His purpose was exposing the ignorance behind such bias. But many local readers didn't get the irony, something I learned during my first weeks of teaching freshman and had confirmed recently with a friend born on a farm not far from Iowa City: unlike people from the coasts, Iowans don't get irony.

Andy took the lead in a much more blatantly disturbing situation. On one of his infrequent socializing nights, a large group of us squeezed into a booth at Kenny's, he was adjacent to the next booth, where three African students were sitting with two blonde undergraduate women. They were just talking when an older man, his tie askew, his coat rumpled, squeezed into their booth. Several of us recognized him—not me—as a well-known Skinnerian psychologist with a major role in devising national college admission aptitude tests.

I was at the opposite end of our booth, not hearing much of what he said, but aware that the man was clearly drunk and belittling. Andy and others, much closer, couldn't miss his words, telling the Africans his power in making up the tests that could, essentially, deny them access. When the psychologist staggered off, Andy organized us all into writing our versions of what we had witnessed over the next few days. He arranged a meeting with the undergraduate dean, a former department colleague of the test-maker, who probably already knew of the man's drinking and biases. The dean didn't go public, but the Skinnerian left for another job at the end of the term.

Beyond Andy's writing obsession was his perfectionism, which may have been an inseparable trait. People reported the tale of him standing on a bridge over the Chicago River and tossing three novel manuscripts into the currents. That was before computers and backup drives. Those pages disappeared scattered in downstream currents. What he did turn out that reached publication were models of craft and precision. He gathered several stories from literary magazines into a thin collection called *To Byzantium* from the University of Illinois Press. Despite a limited output, his stories appeared in *The Atlantic* and *The Norton Anthology of Short Fiction*, among others. His awards included O. Henry Awards, a Guggenheim Fellowship, and one from the National Endowment for the Arts. I wonder what we've all missed in the destroyed work that didn't come up to his standard.

Perhaps he had been additionally traumatized by the fate of his novel, *The Travelers*, based on the actual situation of his Latvian family, where he was one of thirteen children that performed through Europe as the Fetler Family Band, led by his father, Pastor William. According the novel, and probably in fact, the pastor—called Vanya in the novel—chose to seek the favor of the Nazi government as a means of distributing Bibles in the Soviet Union. The children rebelled from the father, though two sons joined the German army. Andy, in contrast, enlisted in the American Army when he arrived in this country from Latvia and was wounded during a battle in Germany. Recovered, he served as a translator.

I recall going to an acceptance party for the novel at Andy and Carol's apartment and what he said to me when I congratulated him as he opened the door: "But what about the reviews?" The eventual reviews were quite positive. What doomed the novel was not the critics but rather than the law's delay. One of his many brothers was teaching at NYU, worried that readers, especially Jewish colleagues and students, would condemn him and his reputation for Nazi complicity. He sued for libel, I believe, to block release of the book by Houghton Mifflin. Eventually, and probably at a significant legal expense for the publisher, the brother lost his case, and Houghton Mifflin lost enthusiasm for publicizing the novel. The sibling antagonism could have been the subject of another novel. Perhaps one was written but never submitted.

Andy had a creative rivalry (or what might have been jealousy) with our Iowa contemporary Richard E. Kim, whom I've written about at greater length in this collection. Kim's novel *The Martyred* came out to unprecedented praise, and I was at a gathering in Andy's apartment during which he attacked the book as an abstract intellectual debate rather than "real" fiction. I tried to defend the novel with reference to Camus' *The Plague*, but Andy wasn't having any of it.

I don't think the personal relationship of the men was actually hostile, just cool, while their wives were great friends. Ironically, both men were both offered teaching positions in the University of Massachusetts-Amherst creative writing program and became colleagues. Andy stayed there until his retirement and remained in the area until his death in March 2017. Carol, whom I liked too, died in 2011.

## Jerry Bumpus

I don't know how I came to know Jerry and don't recall knowing him well. But it must have been well enough for him to offer to store my books when we spent the summer in New York after my first year in Iowa. He and a young woman had an apartment in a house built into a steep hill above a narrow stream. Though it was only a short walk from town, the setting gave it the sense of isolation. Our sublet in New York was a complete contrast, a fifth-floor, tub-in-kitchen walkup on then rundown St. Mark's Place in the East Village, where cockroaches clung like textured wallpaper.

Probably on the afternoon of the book move, several of us walked to the Iowa City zoo, Jerry a bit manic from whatever he had been drinking, grabbing the zoo goat by the horns for a wrestling match. It was a small goat and not much of a challenge. To my surprise, no keepers appeared to break up the tussle. Later, Jerry did write of a Goat Dance. Perhaps this was the inspiration.

Even then Jerry, unlike almost all of us, was already publishing stories, mainly in a literary magazine called *December*, which even turned out his first novel, *Anaconda*. He had another novel and several story collections from various small presses, along with a teaching career at San Diego State, where at least one friend had been his student, with good things to say about him as a man and as a mentor. I did see an online photo of him when he was about forty but felt no echo of recognition. In the fall I did get my books back, and he may have been relieved to be rid of them.

### Glenn Meeter

Glenn came to Iowa with an enviable publication as an *Atlantic* First, that magazine's series of initial appearances by new writers. But Philip Roth, his initial workshop instructor, tore into his new writings in a particularly Rothian manner. (See my own experience in "Roth's Complaint.") Did Roth even give him a C, or is that an apocryphal memory?

Even if Roth did, Glenn seemed unflappable, a solid, well-grounded guy, a man of faith, the least likely person I knew to wrestle with a goat. His wife, Marlene—was it?—came from South Dakota and found Iowa City densely populated and a bit much to cope with. (For me, just a short drive off the two-line highway offered total darkness and more stars in the night sky than I had ever seen before.)

Writing well is the best revenge. And though I can't imagine Glenn as vengeful, I enjoyed a vicarious satisfaction seeing his future list of publications in magazines like *Redbook, Epoch,* and *The Reformed Journal.* We accepted one story when I was editing *The Literary Review.* He also published a novel called *Letters to Barbara* and combined fiction writing with literary scholarship. No surprise there.

### John Yount

A few times in my life I've known people who could do and say outrageous things and get away with them because of sheer charm and likeability. John was one, probably because—in addition—he wasn't mean spirited. In fact, he conveyed a sense that his antics done just for the fun of the challenge. He told of putting a porcupine in a desk drawer of his sergeant when stationed with the army in Germany. While a student at Vanderbilt, mornings he would go out early to shoot a bird and put the carcass in the mailbox of a faculty member just to do it.

John was well known as a hunter and fisherman, often out to bag some game with Vance Bourjaily. I recall John practicing flycasting on the lawn in front of the Iowa Memorial Student Union. He always had a rod in his trunk, ready to jump out and head for a pond or river if he saw a fish break, including the time he amazed locals by catching the legendary and evasive massive trout known as Old Ike.

One day I was about to start a freshman writing class and looked out the classroom door to see a man in jeans and a jean jacket rushing up to the second floor with a cracked open shotgun. John. Of course, today sirens would be blasting and squad cars roaring.

About that freshman class. He found it hard to teach, he said, because he just wanted to say to the young women, "What pretty knees you have." Those words he didn't vocalize, but at the end of a semester, upset by the way students were writing down all that he was telling them, he leaned over the desk with a dark-eyed glare and proclaimed, "Everything I've told you is a lie."

One image that's stuck with me is John knocking at the door or our married-student tin hut late one night during a period when many of us were brewing homemade beer and sake. He was out on a quest for a bottle capper, which we didn't have—just a crock of fermenting raisins in the bathroom. At that time, his then-wife Suzie was pregnant with their first daughter, Jennifer. "You should see, Suzie," he said. "She looks like a kangaroo." (We borrowed that baby's name for our second daughter.)

Probably the traumatic event of John's childhood—which may have been behind his porcupine, dead bird, and Old Ike antics, and which he kept trying to portray in fiction and finally did in one of his novels—was a day when he was five and his father wanted to show off how tough his son was. The father grabbed John by the hair and lifted him off the ground. When the flesh popped from the bone, John cried. His father was disgusted. John talked about that moment often.

John came to Iowa with great hopes for his talent—by faculty and other students— and he began publishing in literary magazines while still in the workshop. Writing caused him great stress, perhaps because he expected so much from himself. He told of stewing over a difficult passage to the point where confronting it made him throw up.

Unlike many writers paralyzed by the fear of failure, John did fulfill his talent to publish five critically acclaimed novels: *Wolf at the Door*, *The Trapper's Last Shot*, *Hardcastle*, *Toots in Solitude*, and *Thief of Dreams*. He received grants from the Rockefeller and Guggenheim Foundations and the National Endowment for the Arts. And he caught Old Ike.

### Frank Chin

Frank I didn't know well, nor did I spend much time in his company. He was living in a small semi-commune house where my then-wife had taken a job as cook for little pay. The person I knew best from the commune members was an undergraduate from Mississippi filled with tales of eccentrics that made me realize Faulkner was more reporting than inventing. Frank, barely in his twenties at that time, was a skinny kid with a guitar. He went on to become an award-winning playwright, a storywriter, and a novelist. A bio note says, "... he is often considered the grandfather of Asian-American literature." His writing success comes as no surprise because it was par for the Iowa course, but "grandfather"? That kid?

## Donald Justice

Unlike the others on this list, Don was a faculty member in his mid thirties during my time at Iowa, though he had been a student earlier, gaining a PhD. When taking graduate lit courses, I heard, he was allowed to submit works emulating the major poets of a period rather than a term paper, though I have no doubt his papers would have been outstanding because he went on to publish essay collections later in his career. Because Paul Engle, the workshop director was not actively teaching, much of the early sixties, Don served pretty much as the entire poetry faculty, which clearly was a plus, considering the major poets who studied with him, including two American poets laureates—Mark Strand and Charles Wright.

He received the Lamont Poetry Prize for *The Summer Anniversaries,* his first book in those years (1961) and was, deservedly, widely liked and admired. His Pulitzer Prize came in 1980.

I don't think I had more than a few brief conversations with Don while a student. Mainly, I kept hearing about him from others who knew him much better, primarily praise for his commitment and generosity to others.

One story revealed a very different side of him. With the American theatre seemingly desperate for plays in the early sixties, Don was one of a group of writers that included Joyce Carol Oates and Philip Roth who received one-year fellowships from, I believe, the Ford Foundation to write scripts. Nothing that resulted was successful, though a few may have had brief productions in tiny theatres. Don, I was told, went back to Florida where he was born, unable to write, and spent much of his time wagering at dog racing tracks. Considering his many poetry collections, he must have needed the discipline of a teaching schedule to focus on his own work.

Don did come to do a talk and a reading on the campus where I was teaching after Iowa, invited by my colleague Bill Zander (more about him later). There, over dinner, he told us more about the parody poetry worksheets produced by Mark Strand, Al Lee, Bill Brown, and perhaps others.

Long before computers and even photocopying, dittos were the means of distributing work to be discussed in workshop sessions, with writers typing their poetry and fiction on forms with a purple gel that came off in backwards letters on a thick second sheet to be attached to a drum for producing multiple copies. Those copies would be inserted into boxes nailed to the metal huts along the Iowa River where classes were held. It was up to students to pick up the week's sheets before class time.

Those parody sheets played up the tics of many student poets and the faculty too. For example, Paul Engle's "In Praise of Iowa Corn" became something like "In Praise of First Street at Avenue A." Although a non-poet, I remember seeing a copy at the time, not knowing enough about the work of those parodied to get the real joke, though I remember hearing some grumbling and upset. Poets had many more rivalries over the schools they belonged to and the techniques they used than fiction writers did. We didn't care how and what others wrote beyond hoping that they did it well and perhaps envying those who succeeded before us.

Don passed on details of some of the consequences of those parodies. Details to follow.

### Edmund Skellings

Ed was considered a character with his constant self-aggrandizing, much of which I suspect was a put-on, a role he played perfectly. People talked about him. Although I never entered the woman's bathroom at Kenny's, I heard about the Skellings graffiti on the walls, the litany of "Ed Skellings is...." I believe "a good lay" was one of the completions, along with another, almost poignant, that said "my husband."

We must have known each other because one day we met on Iowa Avenue during lunch time, both of us seeking a meal, and entered a café to share a booth. I just listened as Ed went on about a school of American poetry in which he and Robert Frost were the only members.

In the parody poetry worksheets, the cruelest blow may have been including one of Ed's poems straight. Yet he did go one to become the poet laureate of Florida and gravitate from his Frost-like period to computer-animated poems shown throughout the U.S., in Tokyo, Berlin, and Madrid, and on PBS. One of his works is titled "The First Electric Poet." Why didn't he tell me his plans at lunch? Perhaps he was keeping his real ambition a secret.

**Richard Lyons**

I've had the help of one of Richie's former MFA students at the University of Oregon in attempting to track down his publications; but both of us came up empty. I do recall hearing over the years about stories of his in magazines. Perhaps they never were collected. He must have had work in print to get tenure at Oregon, when he—like several of my Iowa contemporaries at universities around the country—was hired to start an MFA program.

My most distinct personal memory of him is the trip I and my then-wife took with Richie and his then-wife, Ann, nonstop back east during a break in the Simca they brought back from a trip to France. Those were the days people were buying foreign cars unsuited for driving on American roads. The Lyons Simca was no exception. It blew a head gasket on the return trip.

I do have a vivid memory of the ride to New Jersey for us and Brooklyn for them, trying to contort into a comfortable sleep when I wasn't at the wheel. Yet I have no memory of heading back to Iowa with them or the breakdown. I do remember my ethical dilemma of wondering whether I shared responsibility for the head gasket and should help pay for repair, a dilemma that was moot because I had no money beyond food and rent and a pitcher of beer at Kenny's.

Richie did, despite his Brooklyn origins, become an outdoorsman, forming a close friendship with a non-writer friend of mine, the two of them tramping through fields with rod and reel.

**Earl Ganz**

Earl was another Brookynite, arriving at the Workshop with a story already published in *New World Writing*. He became a founding faculty member of the University of Montana MFA, and went on to publish more stories in good magazines, a collection called *Animal Care* from Lynx House Press (which also did a collection of mine), another collection, and a novel called *The Taos Truth Game*.

Even as a student, his writing was much better than most. But once he showed me a first draft of a story about Barry Goldwater, and I was surprised by the crudity of the prose. He explained that all of his initial versions were similar and that he revised and revised to produce the finished products I admired so much.

While living in New York, to support himself before coming to Iowa, he had worked in a university research lab where his primary duty was euthanizing small mammals for use in scientific experiments. Finally, he couldn't take it and quit, bothered very much by what he had been paid to do. I wonder if the title Animal Care is a gesture of recompense.

His then-wife, Gretchen, at some point took off, literally, to become a bush pilot in Alaska. Of all the many then-wife breakups, to my knowledge, hers was the most dramatic.

Some years after Iowa, when I was editing *The Literary Review*, we published a story of Earl's about a father-daughter conflict that offered so much verisimilitude I could tell it was a sharped report of an actual event, openly confessional. That was at a time before the flourishing of memoir, when autobiography had to be disguised as fiction. Whatever the genre, he wrote it well.

## David Wright

I don't know if Dave ever actually published anything.

Once I sent a long story of his to an editor I knew who wanted to include it in his magazine. But Dave, fearing that the extended family members he fictionalized would see it, withdrew. Still, he wrote as if driven—stories, novels, even a fifty-page letter to the editor of *The Atlantic*.

Even though an Air Force captain, Dave had been given a two-year leave to get an MFA. What that degree had to do with winning wars and keeping the peace, I never understood. Dave lived those two years feverishly, sleeping little, swallowing uppers to squeeze more hours from the day, socializing with intense conversations when he wasn't at his typewriter.

He and his then-wife lived in a real house, unlike almost all the rest of us, afforded by his military pay, with—I believe—four kids, one of whom, an academic daughter, Charlotte, I was in touch with for a while years later. The house was continually packed with family and friends.

Dave was charismatic and compelling, existing at a high pitch of excitement. Even the Air Force must have fallen under his spell. Why else such an extended writing leave?

Born into an Idaho Mormon family, while apostate, he was still obsessed by the religion. It was the source of his fifty-page letter to the editor of the *Atlantic*, driven by a need to correct and clarify something an article in the magazine did or didn't say. On a visit to Wahoo, Illinois, where Joseph Smith had stopped for a time on his way west, Dave stole a doorknob from the Smith house museum. Mormon life was his primary subject.

When Dave's two writing years were up, the Air Force sent him to Vietnam, and he wrote often to me and, I'm sure, a number of others on thin folded and self-sealing letter forms. I doubt they were censored or even screened because what he reported would have been fodder for anti-war protests. Somehow, he established contact with leaders of an ethic mountain tribe and was trying to be a go-between to fulfill a plan to end the war. He became the protagonist of a long, bad novel I wrote called *Worldsaver* that sits on a shelf in typescript unread by human eyes.

When he returned from Vietnam, Dave sent a hurried, distraught message that his marriage was over. His wife had fallen in love with another man while he was away. Not long after I learned Dave had died from a heart attack, still in his late thirties, in part, I suspect, from an emotional broken heart and in part, I also suspect, from swallowing all those uppers.

When I got the news, I was about to publish a paper-back novel, also bad, but was able to dedicate it to the memory of Dave Wright. His daughter told me his family wouldn't allow my novel in the house, judging the bland cover obscene. Then I understood why he had withdrawn that story.

## Marvin Bell

I doubt that Marvin would remember me and I have no recollection of any conversation with him. What I do recall is Marvin at Saturday morning touch football games, crew-cut, wearing a stiff Ridgeway cap, and fulminating about somebody being out of bounds, stamping his feet.

He went on to become a major poet, teaching in the Workshop until retirement, pictured looking sagacious with a long white beard and gaining a reputation for skill and wisdom. All deserved, I'm sure.

But when telling about the parody poetry worksheets,

Don Justice reported Marvin coming to him after seeing his excesses mocked and asking Don if he really wrote that way. Don nodded and agreed that he did. The moment changed Marvin's art and his life. Unlike his touch football anger, his reaction in this case revealed openness and wisdom.

## Robert "Tod" Perry

I don't recall how I got to know Tod or where and when we had conversations. He was a likeable guy with some interesting tales. While an undergraduate at Cornell, he hung out with Thomas Pynchon and Pynchon's roommate, Richard Fariña.

Even in the mid sixties with just the publication of the revolutionary novel *V*, Pynchon was a bit of a legend, unseen and unphotographed. And here was Tod who had been with him almost daily. In fact, he, Pynchon, and Fariña were among a group of students suspended for a student protest at Cornell. After Cornell, the three of them spent time together in New York. This I learned in a 2013 interview I found online.

Fariña had temporary fame, a mixture of celebrity, literary success, and tragedy. Married to Mimi, Joan Baez's sister, when she was just 17, he had published a novel with an engaging title, *Been Down So Long It Looks like Up to Me*, and released two albums sung with Mimi. Then he was killed in a 1966 motorcycle accident in Carmel, California, coming home from a book signing.

In the interview Tod tells of Fariña "roaring thru town arriving at Vance Bourjaily's with a shot deer over the fender, arriving in the dead of winter out of Montana."

With his MFA in poetry, Tod received a job offer from

the University of Puerto Rico, a location that seemed exotically appealing to me after suffering though a number of Iowa winters. But before he boarded the plane on his way to the island, he received a call from the daughter of the department chairman to report that she would be meeting him at the airport because her father was hiding from a student with a gun.

Unlike many of the others I knew at Iowa, Tod's name didn't surface in anything I read or heard about afterward. So, I was glad to learn from the 2013 interview that he had been publishing poems and in 2012 was a winner in the Robert Frost International Poetry Contest. He had been living and operating a business in Germany for many years.

Comparing the writing life at Cornell to that at Iowa, Tod said:

> Finally, going back to the culture at Cornell then, I saw no change in the intensity of talent at Paul Engle's Iowa: Al Lee, Bill Brown, Mark Strand, Annette Basalyga, Donald Justice, Mike Harper, Robert Berner, Phillip Roth, Walter Travis(?), Jerry Bumpus, Jim Crenna, Vern Rutsala (an excellent poet and straight thinker), Tad Richards, there were more, many more plus visits from previous years all friends of the workshop ringmaster Don Justice—Henri Coulette, Phil Levine, Bob Mezey, Chris Wiseman, people like Kim Merker, bars like Irene Kenny's, politicos, musicians, frequent visits by people like Karl Shapiro, WH Auden. Hard to remember so many talents. [...] The poet Charles Wright, and also Steve(?) Parker. And Nick Crome. And for sure Knute Skinner. I hope I have not forgotten other really talented writers [...] I am uneasy about the names of people I forgot to mention. [...] Verlin Cassill (RV Cassill) at Iowa [...] was a faculty writer, always it seemed

involved with Chuck Wright.  I had no classes with him but I was to be found often at the same parties late, late at night.  He was for sure one of the many top fiction people with Bourjaily and Phil Roth.

I had less contact with Morty Marcus and Lew Turco.  I know I met both of them, in Kenny's I recall talking with Lew and also Bill Brady, another good poet.  Morty and Lew were associated with a group of Iowa poets and writers before my arrival, but somehow made extended visits during my time.  I had several good evenings with Morty but Lew I recall meeting only once.

I too knew many of these people beyond those I've written about here. But I can't recall much to say about them. Kim Merker had a long, thick beard and printed books on a handset press. Knute Skinner was emptying a technical writing office desk when I moved in. Nick Crome and I sat next to each other at the graduation ceremony where we received our MFAs—Cr and Cu. I had admired the title of his thesis story collection, "Admit Impediment," from Shakespeare sonnet 116. Chris Wiseman, an English poet, once offered ironic sympathy to fiction writers for all that grunge work of filling pages with words. Al Lee, for a brief time, shared a married student housing unit after the wife left the husband—who was the leader of the student peace organization—for punching her. Tad Richards' living room contained a pyramid of empty Ace Beer cans, seventy-five cents a six pack. Annette Basalyga had been Tod's significant other. She also taught at the University of Puerto Rico, and I assume they went together.

## Mark Strand
Mark was a presence, with the look and posture of an

archetypal poet, carrying himself as if he were already the U.S. Poet Laureate, and I believe it was widely assumed that role was looming in his future even though it didn't exist at the time. He had Major Poet written all over him. I don't recall ever having a conversation with him but did with his then-wife, Antonia, a pleasant woman who did not look the part. She often had their daughter Jessica with her. Stand's poetry reveals a complex inner life that certainly wasn't evident in just looking at him. He socialized with Philip Roth, also a writer of multifaceted alter egos.

### Charles Wright

As Tod Perry noted, he was called Chuck then, but that nickname doesn't seem suitable for yet another American Poet Laureate and Major Poet from the same group at Iowa. Such a laureate coincidence is probably more improbable than lightning striking twice.

Charles came to Iowa after Army service in Italy, where he must have learned the language for his translations and some of his poetic influences. His branch was Army Intelligence, which people referred to as an oxymoron. He played along, soft-spoken, easy, and personable.

Charles, too, we knew was going to be an important poet. That's why what he told the PBS News Hour in 2011 came as a surprise:

> After leaving the Army, by his own account, Wright sort of snuck into the Iowa Writers' Workshop. "My name was on the printout because I'd been accepted to the graduate school and they were sort of loosey-goosey with the program that nobody had bothered to see that I really wasn't on their list. And the rest of course is history."

I wonder how many of us benefitted from those loos-ey-goosey days.

## Mark Costello

For a year or so, Mark and I taught undergraduate Core Lit sections at the same time in the same building. We'd walk across the campus together to wherever we were headed and talk. I don't remember what we talked about—perhaps the lit course or students or writing. I remember him as tall and handsome, although someone who recently discovered his first collection, *The Murphy Stories*, described his look in the cover photograph as "looking louche and sly."

Mark went on to publish a second collection of fiction about the same alter ego character, *Middle Murphy*. Although his output was slight, what there was of it achieved a high standard if not commercial success. Stories were reprinted in Norton anthologies and *The Best American Short Stories*. *The Murphy Stories* did receive the St. Lawrence Award for Short Fiction

He taught at the University of Illinois for many years before retiring. He was first hired in a time where several publications in significant magazines were sufficient for writers to find a position at a major university. Now many with major prizes end up as adjuncts.

A commenter on the Mike Murphy character refers to the character navigating "boyhood shame and sharp-eyed parents, two-bit academic jobs and Catholic guilt, alcoholism and adultery, the Marine Corps and ill-starred marriage." I have no idea how much of Mike was Mark beyond the extremes and distortions of imagination. I do recall hearing his then-wife at Iowa ran off with a best friend. I think Carol Fetler told me that.

## Paul Friedman

Paul also had a career at the University of Illinois and, like Mark, achieved only limited publication despite the excellence of his stories. In both cases, their collections were published by their own university presses. Paul's books are *Serious Trouble* and *And If Defeated Allege Fraud*. Paul, too, obtained his teaching position on the basis of a few stories in prestigious magazines.

I don't recall were it was and how often I sat with Paul and his wife Mary. Perhaps their daughter Story was with them. They were pleasant to be with.

I do recall Paul telling me about being on a train from the east to Iowa City and sitting next to an Iowa farmer, who asked Paul what he did. "I teach writing," Paul told him. The man nodded approvingly. "My son writes a fine hand."

## Philip F. O'Connor

Phil was another person who taught in the same building and at the same time I did. It was late morning, and the two of us went for lunch regularly for much of a semester. What struck me about him then was how non-confrontational he was, even on the most trivial points, avoiding disagreements when the stakes were minimal. For example, he would say something like, "It's a sunny day," and I'd reply, "I hear it's going to rain." And he'd immediately reverse himself: "Yes, it does look cloudy."

A memorial website created after Phil died in 2008 notes, "He refused much praise, took himself out of the running for prizes and devoted much time to encouraging and uplifting others." Others appear to agree he was not assertive, perhaps shy.

That reticence certainly did not impede his success as a writer, with two novels nominated for the Pulitzer Prize— *Defending Civilization* and *Finding Brendan*. His best-selling first novel, *Stealing Home*, was a Book of the Month Club selection. He also published short story collections and served on Pulitzer Prize fiction juries.

Bowling Green University hired him to create an MFA program, the third in the country at that time. Coincidentally, I have a friend who graduated from that program and has nothing but praise for Phil, who was named a Distinguished Professor before he retired.

Because Iowa writer marriages suffered a high failure rate, and because I had introduced Phil to his first wife, Dusty, a friend of friends and a divorcee with a daughter, I asked Phil's former student if Phil and Dusty were still a couple. He didn't know, but the memorial site indicated that they were divorced in 1978 after fifteen years of marriage and five children. Phil married again in 1994 but was divorced again at the time of his death back in his native California.

Once in Iowa, someone told me that Phil, after drinking too much at a party, hit Dusty for dancing with Mark Strand. That may have been a one off, as far as I know. He was a very good writer and an enigma as a man.

### Harry Minetree

I don't know if Harry published much beyond his book on Dr. Denton Cooley, the most famous heart surgeon of the time and the first to implant an artificial heart. Harry revered him because Cooley had operated on his heart when Harry was barely into his twenties. I can't say if Cooley literally saved his life, but Harry certainly assumed he had.

He probably was right. A 1969 news story in a local Missouri paper reported that Harry's first surgery for a congenital heart defect failed. According to him, "My prognosis was dismal." He became the first Cooley patient to have a defective aorta replaced by a Dacron substitute.

The paradox was that after escaping serious cardiac danger and, young as he was, having fathered a brood of babies and toddlers with his equally young wife, Judy, he drank himself in a stupor many nights and was usually tipsy on the others.

I recall visits with the Minetrees to the apartment of a friend who dropped out of the MFA program and his not-too-bright then-wife, Loretta, from the Bronx, who insisted that we all take off our shoes before entering the apartment and delivered ongoing malapropisms and absurdities. For example, she said the wife of another student belonged to some strange religion, "like a Seven Day Adventurist." She also, when baking a pie thought, "Shortening—that's the same as butter, isn't it?" This, while her husband recited long passages from Joyce's *Ulysses* from memory.

What Loretta lacked in wit she made up for in pulchritude, mainly prominent breasts in torpedo bras. In his cups, Harry would lurch toward them with hands opened into claws, while Judy giggled and squealed in a Southern drawl, "Now leave Loretta alone." Harry never did make contact, at least not when I was there.

That same 1969 newspaper article reports that, with an advance from Little, Brown, Harry, Judy, and their five children were sailing to London for a year when he would write the book. He did, which must have called for focus and sobriety. (The kids, by the way, all had nicknames much like Poogin and Pidi and Wawa. I wonder what they're called now in middle age.)

## James Crenner

The last time I saw Jim was at an MLA conference after he had received his PhD from Iowa, and I learned he had interviewed with the chair of my department but probably would take a position at Hobart, which offered a lighter teaching load. It turned out to be a good choice because he ended up with an endowed chair and co-founded *The Seneca Review* with Ira Sadoff. I would have enjoying having him as a colleague.

In addition to poems in many magazines, he's published two collections—*The Aging Ghost* and *My Hat Flies on Again*. I've found, though a search, that Marvin Bell is cited as telling the story of Jim being nervous about sitting for his PhD orals and asking Marvin to wait nearby, Marvin then learning from the committee chair that Jim's orals performance was, in the chair's experience, second to only Don Justice's.

At Iowa Jim lived in a Quonset hut in a married student housing compound with his then-wife, Kate, and several babies and toddlers. I remember visiting briefly and feeling very cramped under the rounded ceilings. My own dwelling also was army surplus tin but at least with straight walls.

While Jim was living in the Quonset, *Life* magazine sent the famous photographer Alfred Eisenstaedt to do a spread on the Iowa Workshop. The result convinced me to always be skeptical about photojournalism. For example, Eisenstaedt arranged a class session on a grassy bank of the Iowa River, the students all wearing colorful clothing. But classes never met outside on the riverbank, no matter how photogenic such a scene would have been. In Jim's case, Eisenstaedt had Jim and Kate string clothesline all across their Quonset and drape it with washed diapers, again something that never happened in real life. In that pre-Pampers era, even as poor as we all were, we could afford diaper services.

## Michael Culross

Mike was a friend of Jim Crenner's, although I don't remember how they knew each other. And when Mike transferred to Iowa, he was an undergraduate, although he did eventually get a Workshop degree and publish poems, including the collection *The Lost Heroes* from the Pitt Poetry series. Unfortunately, he died of cancer in 2011.

Several weeks into a semester, Mike appeared in a Core Lit class I was teaching, the only bright spot in the group. Until then, it had been a dismal group. My method at the time was to prepare a list of discussion questions about the day's readings and ask for responses. The silences were agonizing, me constantly fretting at the front of the room as I tried to reformulate: "Let me ask in another way." I'm sure the students shared the agony.

In fact, a group of young women came to my office. They had heard the other Core Lit section I was teaching that term was so lively and energetic, so good. What was wrong with our section? How could I tell them, "It's you. The people in the other class are brighter"? And they were, far more alert, responding to my list of questions in half the class time, the rest available for engaging free association.

Mike's arrival changed everything, and I fear most of

the rest of the semester involved a conversation between the two of us, the others rarely participating. I suppose I should be considered a failure as an instructor. But I did escape excruciating hours.

## William Zander

I almost left Bill off this list, mainly because I didn't think of him as just an Iowa person. He has been an ongoing friend and presence in my life since 1961 when he appeared to take a desk in the technical writing instructors' office, a tall, very thin young man with a standup crew-cut. That's more than fifty years ago. When he left Iowa to return to the University of Missouri, I visited Columbia, Missouri, a few times, and he came back to Iowa City to visit, sampling the homemade sake a number of us were fermenting and sleeping on the sofa.

When my department had an opening for a poet, I encouraged Bill to apply and accept the offer. He occupied my house and cared for our dog when I spent six months in England during my first sabbatical. The next fall, when he was in Spain on his, I with family visited him in Deja, Mallorca, over the Christmas holidays. But, in keeping with the focus of these vignettes, I'll limit my memories to Bill in Iowa City and the suburb of Coralville, where he and his then-wife, Sara Lee, lived in the basement flat of a house owned by a medical student with a two-year-old son who constantly played with himself, to his parents' alarm and embarrassment.

Bill and Sara Lee shared that flat with an orange tomcat called Philip (really Philly Joe Jones), who sought out fierce confrontations with rats, returning home with bites and torn ears, and not infrequent visits to vets. Bill liked to name things. His car at the time was a ponderous, wallowing pale green DeSoto that he dubbed Henry James. Later, when he taught creative writing, he told his students to call the course Otto, influenced by John Lennon answering "George" when asked what he called his haircut. Bill also was far ahead of other musical critics when he published an essay on the genius of the Beatles a year ahead of Richard Poirier's much more influential article in *The Partisan Review*.

Beyond writing poetry with Don Justice and fiction with Verlin Cassill, Bill played the guitar and wrote songs (my favorite of his lyrics lines comes from "When It's Summertime in Maine"—"When the bougainvillea blooms / we will look for furnished rooms). He also sketched very well and once gave me a book of his drawings that included the elaborate carved-framed Victorian mirror behind the bar at Donnelly's, an occasional alternative to Kenny's. Bill also possessed an encyclopedic knowledge of jazz. Who else could refer to the clarinetist Alcide "Yellow" Nunez in a work of fiction as if the reader should know who that was?

But beyond writing, Bill's greatest passion then and still now is fishing. He introduced me to a fixation on the quest for bites, spending hours on the edge of the Coralville Reservoir or the banks of the Iowa River. We bought lures and bait at Cliff Hoag's tackle shop, where Cliff kept a large spoon-billed paddlefish in a tank. When we bemoaned our lack of catches, Cliff alternated explanations—"The water's too warm" or "The water's too cold."

Bill in the Coralville flat owned a black and white TV (we had none), where we would, with our then-wives, watch among the very limited offerings 1930's gangster movies that we called "You Sap" movies because of that term's frequent use in dialogue.

Whenever I read one of Bill's poems—he has two collections, *Distances* and *Gone Haywire and other Old Sayings*—I can hear his voice and see many of the details of people and places. Yet those poems possess a wonder that transcends the man I know and the many hours we've spent together.

## Afterword: Walter Cummins

My wife challenged me to write about myself back then as if the words were someone else's memory. The task may be impossible. I've had many experiences of reuniting with friends from my past and remembering things they did or said that come as complete surprises to them. While those memories stir no recognition in the listener, they are central to the picture of the person I've carried with me all those years. And, I have to assume, vice versa.

The best I can do in this case is try to step outside myself and reconstruct who I think another person would have seen. As I look back on this collection of memories of so many others and the time I must have spent with such a range of people—as well as non-writer friends—I wonder how I ever accomplished anything else. Yet I was a driven student—reading books, writing academic papers, preparing to teach, grading student papers, struggling at story and novel writing, eventually helping to care for two babies.

One answer may be that Iowa City was such a compact community, nothing more than a few minutes away from anything else. No time wasted commuting from place to place. You could pack multiple activities into a single day: read, write, teach a class, attend a class, change a diaper or two, lunch with a friend, hang out for an evening hour or two at Kenny's, even fish a few times a week.

But how would someone remember me? I certainly wasn't one of the student writers famed for the certainty of becoming famous, or at least creatively successful. Charles Wright's "loosey goosey" explains to me how I got into the Workshop. Other than two embarrassing paperback novels, I didn't start regularly publishing short stories till ten years after receiving an MFA. A late starter, and I've never won a major award. (Some minor ones, though.)

Maybe others thought of me as that guy who occupied a chair in a Workshop classroom or a booth at Kenny's, who drove a faded blue antique VW Beetle that wouldn't start in winter temperatures, who caught a fish or two.

I did have a reputation as a good student, at least by certain lit faculty, getting A's on the long essays I had no trouble churning out, taking electives in intellectual history and philosophy. After a mediocre undergraduate career, I revealed myself to myself as a literary intellectual. In anyplace but Iowa City, that might have sufficed. But I was there to be a writer. What did an A in a Dickens seminar matter if I couldn't produce a publishable short story?

People often ask what I learned about writing at Iowa, and all I can come up with is a few anecdotal pieces of advice, Verlin Cassill suggesting that I sit myself in a dark corner and contemplate how to come up with an ending for a story that badly needed one. He was serious. I'm sure there must have been other useful revision recommendations for long-forgotten stories and a novel that never amounted to much.

So what did I come away with from five years in Iowa City, several degrees, and the experience of fiction workshops? When I left town for a life back East in a new red

VW Beetle, with possessions stuffed under the front hood and two relatively new kids in the back seat? I certainly had read a lot, turned out praised essays, gained teaching experience, produced pages of inadequate fiction, and—perhaps most important—I got to know all the people I've told about here and many more. I was part of a community that mattered with people who still matter.

But none of this addresses the challenge of imagining what others would have said about me as my young Iowa City avatar. Would anyone—unlike me—remember anything I wrote back then? Did I ever say or do anything memorable or clever? Or would they just wonder, "Whatever happened to that guy called Cummins?"

"Who?"

# Kennedy and Kerrigan in Copenhagen

I can't review *Kerrigan in Copenhagen*, ostensibly because the novel's author, Thomas E. Kennedy—Tom—is a good friend, and a review by me might appear compromised. But, beyond that, and more crucial, is the fact that it's impossible to read the work with any sense of aesthetic distance, something I can do with novels by other friends, even those by Tom. But my encounter with *Kerrigan in Copenhagen* is in many ways a reentry into material I already know well— Tom himself, the city as experienced during brief visits, the real people whom I've met in person and appear as walk-on characters, the jazz musicians whose records I've heard and whose lives I know about, the familiar references to writers and literary history, and details of events from Tom's life. Most of these biographical particulars came from live and email conversations with Tom or from other shorter works—stories and essays—he has written about these subjects. Reading *Kerrigan in Copenhagen*, I often envision real people instead of the creations on the page, Tom Kennedy instead of Terrence Kerrigan, aware of the actual events that served as sources of many of the fictional events in the novel.

That's not to say that much of the novel isn't new to me, mainly some of the invented life of the title character, or more precisely the backstory of that life, the trauma that occurred before the novel's present. I had read the first published version (from Wynken de Worde in Galway), with a slight difference in title, *Kerrigan's Copenhagen*, a decade ago. But this incarnation is the result of significant cuts, brief substitutions of new material, and most importantly, a very different reason for Kerrigan's psychic wounding, which is even more convincing and effective. Tom and I had a number of email discussions about these revisions while he was in the midst of making them, so I had an overall sense of what I'd find, just not the specific manifestations.

Given the T.E.K. initials, it's hardly a secret that Terrence Einhorn Kerrigan is a Kennedy doppelgänger, sharing many personal details, favorite books and music, friends, and love of Copenhagen, as well as intimate knowledge of the city's geography, history, philosophers, musicians, artists, and writers. The streets, the buildings, and the serving houses are also real, and the novel could enjoy a parallel existence as a walking and drinking tour guidebook. I've been to many of the places with Tom, seen the bullet hole in Rosengaarden Bodega and erotic ceiling fresco in The Booktrader, listened to live Dixieland in the White Lamb (*Det Hvid Lam*), heard recorded Cannonball Adderley from speakers in The Fiver, and enjoyed a meal in the Spicy Kitchen, though Kerrigan just walks past this time.

So, although Kennedy is not Kerrigan, their lives run on some parallel tracks, knowing the same people, reading the same books, sharing experiences in Manhattan, California, Fort Dix, Dublin. Kerrigan's reactions to Joyce's *Ulysses*, Coltrane's "My Favorite Things," and Arnold's "Dover Beach" are Kennedy's.

But, Kerrigan differs significantly from Tom with his fictional parents, ex-wife, and child, lack of literary success, and, most crucially, a personal drama that provides an oppressive weight to the story. He exists as an alter ego conjured by Tom during a dark night of the soul.

The initial version of the novel was celebrated for offering a Copenhagen that's an equivalent of Joyce's Dublin in *Ulysses*, a city that also appears in this novel as a travel diversion of Kerrigan. That's no surprise because Tom frequently notes his affection for and debt to Joyce and has written extensively about his own visits to Dublin. Both writers share the fixation for precise details, Joyce recreating his city from exile, famously writing letters to verify matters like the height of the fence at 7 Eccles Street. Tom, fortunately, only had to walk out his door to conduct a similar piece of research, if the facts weren't already engrained in his memory.

A primary difference is that Joyce reveals much about Dublin along the way, in a sense, because that is where *Ulysses* takes place, and Joyce feels no need to introduce or explain. Kerrigan, in contrast, is not a native of Copenhagen, knowing much but engaged in ongoing research that provides the ostensible present action of the novel as he prepares to write a guidebook to the city's 1500-plus serving houses, supported in a great degree by his alluring Danish Associate and her encyclopedic Moleskine notebook. Many of their conversations are a form of accumulating knowledge, what she knows about a place and its history supplemented by what he knows that she doesn't. Together they provide a comprehensive portrait of Copenhagen's past and present, of its geography, of the famous people who lived there, and ultimately of their own place in that portrait.

Tom Kennedy has similar inclinations to explore and document in a fascination for the location of famous lives.

He too enjoys pointing out and even photographing the former dwelling places of and monuments to writers and artists in Copenhagen—Kierkegaard, Andersen, and Georg Brandes—and beyond—Descartes, Verlaine, and Hemingway in Paris; Alan Ginsberg, Theodore Dreiser, Marianne Moore, and Edna St. Vincent Millay in New York. What for Kerrigan is a form of obsession is for Tom a happy literary avocation.

I've participated by literally following Tom's footsteps—our literary pub crawl of Manhattan several years ago that included The White Horse (made famous by Dylan Thomas but a gathering spot for dozens of writers over the years, though during our stop it was overrun by a fife and drum corps from Scotch Plains, New Jersey); Pete's Tavern, where we sat at the table where O. Henry wrote; and Chumley's before it closed down, where books and book jackets of its author patrons abounded. Inspired by a gathering of expatriate writers Tom arranged in Paris' Left Bank Place de la Contrescarpe—Ellen Hinsey, David Applefield, Lauren Davis, Ethan Gilsdorf, Dave Poe, the late Janet McDonald—we initiated an online series of writings and photographs about our literary travels called *The Literary Explorer* for Web Del Sol (literaryexplorer.webdelsol.com). Would that Kerrigan enjoyed as much pure pleasure from his flaneur-like wanderings.

What's brilliantly inventive about *Kerrigan in Copenhagen* is the integration of such information with plot and emotion. Kerrigan's research is not merely an excuse for a history lesson, as fascinating as that lesson may be. Rather, the information is inseparable from the man and the way he thinks, his way of coping with the disruption of his life, but also his way of orienting that life into the context of the history and culture around him. Although Kerrigan may be psychically isolated, his greatest quest is to place himself and his personal story in a much broader perspective of human history and to find a way to connect.

Existentialism, with roots in Kierkegaard, seems pertinent. Kerrigan belongs in that category, even though he may have gone to his mother's funeral and certainly shot no one on a beach under a scorching sun. He is very much *de trop*, unmoored, living in a foreign land, trying to immerse himself in the reality of a place, desperate to transform existence into essence.

He constantly associates the timing of real and fictional events by date, eventually relating them to his own life; for example: "In 1821 John Keats died at the age of twenty-four, the same year Dostoyevsky and Flaubert were born, two years after the birth of Melville and Whitman in 1819, which was six years after the birth of Kierkegaard in 1813, the year the Danish State went bankrupt, six years after the Duke of Wellington bombarded Copenhagen killing nearly 2 percent of its civilian population...," eventually leading to Kierkegaard writing *The Seducer's Diary* in 1843, one hundred years before Kerrigan was born and 145 years before he was seduced by his ex-wife, Licia. The chain of history usually returns to what happened to Kerrigan.

The social, cultural, artistic, literary, and Kerrigan personal history all meld in a sea of allusion, the prose itself offering a manic density of thoughts and references, in a rush of sentences that, while not quite Joycean stream of consciousness, reveal rich associations of Kerrigan's mind. While the music of the prose gives pleasure to the reader, what it contains is a torment for the man who is its source. Consider:

> For a moment he thinks he loves her and will propose marriage, but quickly dismisses the thought, knowing that it would involve other people, too, her daughters, witnesses, officials. In any event, marriage will do nothing to alleviate this pinpoint of death fear. It is all illusion, delusion, and the job of human beings is to maintain that delusion in order to enjoy themselves and accomplish their work upon this earth: to live and be happy and love the heady liquor of the drink known as air, and that, anyway, is something. The word *delusion* is immediately accompanied in Kerrigan's mind by an image of Licia in her bikini blue as the false blue of her eyes.

Knowledge is never an end in itself. Kerrigan connects the details of his own failed marriage with the actual story of Kierkegaard and Regine Olsen, the empty love life of Hans Christian Andersen, the delusions of Goethe's young Werther, wondering if Lotte lured the poor suicide on. He broods over the dangerous rages of Stan Getz, the inability of musical genius to save him from himself. The failures of his own life drive him to dwell on those of others.

Kerrigan's visits to the city's serving houses are hardly passive, for he is a very active drinker—from beer to wine to absinthe, frequently overindulging, as expert on hangovers as he is on drinking. He notes two kinds, one of a head shaken with hammering and sawing, "the other kind for agonizing, the moral sort." Yet he is driven to seek the comforts of alcohol mixed with sexual hunger, specifically for his Associate. Will either fill the vacancy within? Even with her, Kerrigan having consumed three frog-green glasses of absinthe, thoughts of Licia invade his mind, and the Associate has to bring him back to the present: "Hey, Terrence," she whispers, "you're not alone." But he is, page after page.

On the novel's first page, which opens with the announcement that he is in love with Copenhagen, several paragraphs later the reader is told:

> Here he will clothe himself in its thousand years of history, let its wounds be his wounds, let its poets' songs fill his soul, let its food fill his belly, its drink temper his reason, its jazz sing in the ears of his mind, its light and art and nature and seasons wrap themselves about him and keep him safe from chaos.

Will it keep him safe, provide a safe harbor for his tormented mind? That question is what the novel is about, the unknown that substitutes for a conventionally plotted story of what will happen next. More wandering, more drinking, more learning, more talking, more sex, real and hoped for, accumulate as he moves about the city. But where will he end up, finally at home or condemned to live out his life as a faux Danish version of the Wandering Jew? Both Andersen and Kierkegaard, men who did not like each other, as Kerrigan reveals, used the legendary character, Andersen making Ahasuerus the Angel of Doubt, while Kierkegaard made him the basis of his essay "The Unhappiest One." Will Kerrigan be yet another version?

For all of Kerrigan's extensive knowledge, all that he knew before his research and all that he learns from it, his constant concern is whether information compensates for the fundamental ignorance that has blighted his life. Licia's bitter accusation, "You are so blind," haunts him, and he wonders if the Associate used the same words during drug-enhanced sex. She claims not to remember.

Author biography is of little use in *really* reading a

literary work, though I can understand why people have deep curiosity about the personal histories of the favorite writers, along with actors, politicians, and sports heroes. But these are of a piece with the *People* magazine mentality, and they can be misleading and distorting. Celine and Pound and Hamsun were Nazi sympathizers. That may be at the back of our minds when we engage their work, ruining the experience. But the work is not the man or the woman; literary biography can only document the raw material.

What emerges from the writer's hand or keyboard or dictation has a life of its own, the facts of experience like the seeds of flowers planted each spring. A transformation begins in dirt, emerges into the light, and can bloom with great beauty. While interviews with writers attempt to fathom how that revelation happens, the results are technical details inadequate to the task. The essence of the real creativity is a mystery.

For all the hours of conversation and thousands of emails, not once did I hear the language and rhythms and music of Tom Kennedy's writings. In fact, I'd say the same about all the writers and poets I have spent time with because I'm just interacting with the person, the external self, not the creative center that is never directly accessible.

Because Tom shared the steps of his writing process, the number of words cut, the number added, I knew early on that he had invented a new backstory to replace the more extreme circumstance in the novel's first appearance a decade before. So Licia, who has abandoned Kerrigan and vanished with their child, is just a literary device. And yet as she is embodied in the book's language, envisioned in her blue bikini and with her deceiving blue eyes again and again, I can't help but suspend my disbelief and consider her cruelly real, grieving along with Kerrigan for his victimization by treacherous false love and for the loss of the child he will never see again. As much as I'm aware Licia is a pure fabrication, I'm unable to resist. "He has been thinking about her for years," we're told, "and still she is not finished with him."

Arnold's "Dover Beach" gains great significance as the novel ends. Is the world "a darkling plain / Swept with confused alarms of struggle and flight"? or can lovers "be true / To one another"? Long before reading this version of the novel, I knew the details of the near encounter with dying in the penultimate chapter and the Associate's revelation in the final one. As a consequence, not surprised, I have no way of telling how other readers will react to the story's resolution.

Aware of so much about the world and people and events of *Kerrigan in Copenhagen*, I can't engage with the novel as pure reading experience. I read and remember simultaneously, juggling the flourishings of imagination with their seed-like sources. Yet page after page I am in awe of the writing and the invention, wondering how my friend did it.

# Riding the Dog: A Look Back at America
## *by Thomas E. Kennedy*

At a time of economic collapse and political failure [2008], many Americans are bewildered by the upheaval of values and identity—who we are as a people, what has shaped us, and what lies ahead. Although they are not meant as social or political analysis, the six essays in Thomas E. Kennedy's *Riding the Dog: A Look Back at America* may provide more profound insights than theoretical speculations by the official pundits. These imaginative evocations of people, landscapes, history, and personal experience offer vivid revelations of what it means to live in the United States.

Tom Kennedy enjoys a unique perspective for writing about America. He has spent half his life in Europe, primarily Denmark, and has traveled throughout the world. But he retains his American citizenship and makes frequent trips back to the U.S., staying in close contact with family and his many friends in this country. This international context enriches his observations. His writer's voice, his eye for the exact detail, and sense of craft make these essays works of literature, not just journalistic observations.

Because of my long friendship and collaborations with Tom Kennedy, I can't pretend to be an objective reviewer. I knew several of these essays while they were in progress and a few even before they were written. But rather than recluse myself from talking about the book, I accepted the invitation to comment. The quality of the essays need no defense. Five were nominated for Pushcart Prizes, three receiving honorable mention, and one reprinted in *New American Essays*. Kennedy also has won, for another essay, the 2008 National Magazine Award. That's in addition to the many stories, novels, reviews, translations, and more that have made him a significant writer. Consider what I have to say here an appreciation rather than an evaluation.

The title essay, "Riding the Dog," is a masterpiece for its depiction of the profound chasm of class, income, and education in America. The dog is a Greyhound bus, and the people who ride it are there because they cannot afford plane fares or car travel. Some of the men have served jail time, some of the passengers lack teeth or jobs, some are physical wrecks, some literally confused as to where they are, especially a young man named Marvin, just out of the prison he entered at sixteen, constantly needing reassurance that he is on the right bus to his wife and two young daughters he "loves ... to death." All desperate for some breaks, living hand to mouth, they exist in a very different cultural world from the author. Kennedy becomes Marvin's guide, getting him to his destination, where Marvin rides off in the crowded family Ford and Kennedy joins waiting friends in the "redolent black leather seat" of a Mercedes SUV.

In the Savannah bus station, Kennedy thinks of names from the world he knows, people who have lived in the same state—Conrad Aiken, Johnny Mercer, Flannery O'Connor, Martin Luther King, Julliette Gordon Low. Passing signs for Paris Island, his memories turn to writers who served in the Marines and to the legacy of Vietnam. Yet the effect is not superiority over what the others on the bus for their igorance, but rather empathy. Their lives matter. Their human needs and wants transcend their informational limitations.

"In the Dark," a tale of coping with the New York blackout of August 2004 is much funnier, at least in parts, especially Kennedy's fierce search for a flashlight for his climb to a room on the 21$^{st}$ floor of the rundown Hotel Carter, but also his brief encounters with an Estonian exchange student, an Irish barmaid, a cabdriver of indeterminate origins, and others maneuvering through the dark. But poignant and disturbing is the refusal of a Plaza Hotel doorman named Washington to serve a glass of water to the thirsty child of a young woman of color who has carried her daughter for a 100-block walk.

"The Bridge Back to Queens," at its core a homage to Kennedy's father, is alive with memories of a personal and a neighborhood past, the elders all gone now, the shops replaced by the businesses of other ethnic groups, *ubi sunt* the essay's mantra. As in the other essays, Kennedy enriches the piece with references to writers and musicians, particularly those who lived in Queens—Bix Beiderbecke, Louis Armstrong, Dizzy Gillespie, Simon & Garfunkel—but mainly John Cheever as written about by his daughter Susan, who often walked with him to the middle of the Queensboro Bridge and who is honored by her in a way Kennedy wishes he could honor his father. But, of course, he has done that in this essay.

Kennedy's involvement with the writers who have informed and even changed his life serves as the primary subject of "Land Where Our Fathers Wrote," the description of the walk through Manhattan to the one-time homes of famous authors, some memorialized by plaques, others who should be—Allen Ginsberg, Marianne Moore, e.e. cummins, Theodore Dreiser, Edna St. Vincent Millay, Ted Joans, O. Henry, Antoine de Saint Exupéry, Gregory Corso, Dylan Thomas, Mark Twain, Bob Dylan, and many others, including the long list of those who drank and left copies of their books in Chumley's bar on Bedford Street. Emma Lazarus lived at 18 East 10th Street, and her words—"Give me your tired, your poor, / Your huddled masses yearning to be breathe free" —are probably better known in the world than those of any of the others, though possibly not Bob Dylan, who gave voice to upheavals of an earlier decade.

In "Bailing Out in Peoria," Kennedy reveals his failure to complete a cross-country bicycle ride to San Francisco in 1967, after dropping out of City College, justified by the many writers who didn't have college degrees—Steinbeck, Faulkner, Hemingway, Salinger, Kerouac. An equally strong motivation is his desire to leave the borough of Queens and the ghost of his recently dead father. With his unlikely traveling partner, a tough ex-jock and NRA member named Nick, a man in great shape for cycling, Kennedy agonizes up hills, trembles through packs of snarling mutts, and sleeps in a tent pitches in mud. Mixed with these physical tortures are mental tortures, haunting memories of his father's failures. In Peoria, Kennedy gives up—sells his bike and hitchhikes to a disappointing San Francisco, taking a bus back to New York the next morning. His own failure, the quitting, lies inside him "like a wound." Though the essay reveals an intensely personal story, it is emblematic of the failure of dreams in America, the inability to pass through "the golden door" promised by Emma Lazarus.

In "Life in Another Language," the concluding essay, political and cultural comparison becomes the overt subject, life in America compared with life in Denmark. The essay begins with a litany of American weaknesses—its racism, its death penalty, its homophobia, its violence, its narrow-minded legacy. Yet Kennedy also criticizes the country he now lives in—growing intolerance of immigrants, xenophobia, right-wing government. Still, its long-tradition of openness, its free higher education and free medical care that justify the high taxes, and its self-irony and "humanistic view of life" make Denmark for Kennedy his country of preference: "I don't think I could bear to leave Copenhagen for more than the few visits I make to the States each year."

While every reader of *Riding the Dog* might not make the same choice, all will come away with a deeper comprehension of life in this country by sharing the experiences and vision of one very talented writer with the power to tell us what it means to be an American.

# *Deciphering and Creating Identities: Peter Selgin,* The Inventors

Most writers spend hours brooding over an idea they feel compelled to turn into story form, usually a subject stemming from a seminal or even traumatic life experience. They contemplate a strategy for presenting it, sometimes over many years. They may eventually put words on a page or even complete an entire draft. A handful may even produce a published book, and even fewer turn out a work that can be called literature.

Such is the case of Peter Selgin's *The Inventors*, material contemplated for quite a while, resulting in a novel draft and earlier memoir versions, as well as being touched upon directly and in disguise in several short stories. He was immersed in a process of discovery and rediscovery, shaping and reshaping, selecting and organizing until he finally produced the successful book he had hoped to achieve from his earliest inklings.

I'm fortunate to have at least two of the earlier attempts on my hard drive to compare with the published result. I'm also fortunate that Peter has been a long-time friend, from the time he was a writer of exceptional promise, through his earliest publications, to a Flannery O'Connor prize-winning story collection, a novel, an essay collection, two books on the craft of fiction, and many excellent stories and essays that have seen that initial promise more than fulfilled.

In addition to reading those previous drafts, I also have spoken with Peter about the people and events that have compelled his imagination. That makes me too much an insider of the circumstances of the memoirs making to be an objective reviewer. But I am able to reflect on the creative processes that resulted in *The Inventors*.

The memoir focuses on two men who were central to the author's life, one a teacher first encountered for just a few years during Peter's early adolescence, but who became an unforgettable and haunting presence long after. Not only did Peter ponder him often as an adult, he even made a cross-country trip a seek him out. That journey and adventure around it became the subject of a completed manuscript. In addition, the teacher was fictionalized in a novel called *The Man in Blue,* in which the teacher is called Jack Thompson. The actual person was a dominating personality, at first a guru and role model, yet also a source of mystery in the uncertainty of his background and the tales he told about himself.

Who was he really? Peter announces his difficulties in writing about the man, in capturing the essence of his character and their relationship: "For years I've tried to write about the teacher, to make our relationship comprehensible—as opposed to classifiable or categorical—to disinterested parties." Even in the final version, his notebook pages faint in the sunset, he admits that he's writing in the dark and that digging up the corpse of the past "is a job best undertaken by night."

The other man, with a seemingly very different role in Peter's life, his father Paul, was a constant presence from Peter's birth to the man's death when his son was an adult. He is the literal inventor of the memoir's title, a brilliant, idiosyncratic personage who turned out important devices in a cluttered backyard barn workshop, while behaving with many obvious quirks. He, too, as his son learns when his father is no longer alive, was also a man of mystery. Much of his personal history was a fabrication.

Both men share the central fact of inventing their lives, at least the lives they projected to those around them. There's also a question of what they actually believed about themselves, how much they were convinced by their own deceptions.

Yet the final memoir brings in a third inventor, the author himself, in two senses. The most essential for any writer, particularly one of a memoir, is what is actual and what made up. Because Peter writes so effectively, his telling becomes convincingly authentic. But the book concludes with an afterword by his twin brother, George, who contradicts many of the specifics in the previous pages. George grew up in the same house but remembers differently. Few memoir writers have twins, but most know someone who witnessed the same events. They don't invite those others to question their memories between the same covers.

But the invitation to his brother is much more than a clever device by the author. Rather it lies at the core of the book, which is about the invention of lives—all our lives, not just those of exposed fabricators. More than giving an opposing voice to George, Peter makes himself a third conundrum in *The Inventors*, revealing himself to the point where he confesses a weakness that destroyed his relationship with the mother of his daughter. Unlike the teacher and the parent who escaped into secrets, he tries to be very open as he intersperses autobiographical scenes and memories not directly connected with the teacher or his father, including a number about his relationship with his twin, a subject he deliberately avoided in earlier works. Yet, the question remains. How much has he invented himself? How much have I? You?

This question hasn't been left hidden in the pages of the book, awaiting the epiphany of an alert reader. Quite the opposite. It's announced in a one-page prologue that didn't exist in earlier versions:

> We inhabit fictional narratives that we come to think of as "our lives." From memories, sifted, sorted, selected, or synthesized—consciously or unconsciously—we assemble the stories that tell us who we are. In that sense, we're all inventors.

# Americans' Anger: H. L Hix

> "I've got a family to feed, a neighborhood to
>   defend."
> "I've got a family to feed, a principle to defend."
> "I've got a family to feed, my honor to defend."

> — H.L. Hix, *American Anger*

These lines taken from separate poems in the first section—"Aggression Cues"—of H. L. Hix's 2016 poetry collection, *American Anger: An Evidentiary*, can serve as elements of a mantra for the entire book. The voice behind the statements speak to the sense of threat perceived by many. Beyond their jobs at stake, they abstract their personal vulnerability to a widening circle of community, values, and integrity. Those threatened feel a need to strike back at the people—e.g., immigrants—and forces—e.g., the economic-political system—they believe are undermining their lives. The section ends with this couplet:

> As when one citizen, perceiving aggression
> from another, behaves aggressively in return.

Some may believe that anger in America originated with the candidacy of Donald J. Trump—what with his podium exhortations to throw the bum out or beat up protesters. But Trump merely tapped into a tendency boiling beneath the surface of our national mentality for many years. His candidacy, of course, exacerbated it, expanded its range, and even gave it legitimacy for millions. Anger erupted and he won his party's nomination. Was that his strategy or just an accident of timing? Was he a candidate with the right message at the right time? Note that his message of not just an American phenomena. Millions in the United Kingdom voted for Brexit. Right-wing parties in many European countries exploit economic insecurities, the possible danger of ISIL, thousand of immigrants, and fear of the looming Other.

But Hix in *American Anger* concentrates on the American manifestations of such ire in poems that capture visceral aspects of this violent urge but also explore causes and the nature of anger itself. Most commentators offer a socio-economic analyses of that anger, finding its source in the frustrations of a cohort of middle-aged blue collar white males whose jobs have disappeared, whose income has shrunk, who feel displaced and threatened by people of color, who blame outsourcing and immigration, who conflate their feelings of lost personal power with lost national prestige and threats of terrorism. But there are also angry woman, even beyond the wives of the men, and angry people making a decent living. They crave a hero who will fight back to restore all that they have lost. A self-proclaimed winner who will make them winners again.

They can't acknowledge that the remedies proposed are simplistic: build a wall, round up and deport millions, seal off borders, reject immigrants, bring back well-paying jobs, let other countries pay their way and stop adding to our national debt. But primarily, kick ass. It feels so good.

As much as many actions of the angry manifest as destructive and self-destructive, the motivations behind the hostile shouts, tee shirts, posters, and bumper stickers reveal a deep sense of threat to their employment, their children's futures, their values, and the core of their lives. They want to strike out because they feel themselves powerless, and they actually are, overwhelmed by social and economic forces far beyond their control. But how to protest against abstractions? Carrying a placard that says, "Ban Robotics" is far less tangible and personified than one that says of Hillary Clinton, "Lock Her Up!" Yet the angry have some justification for their frustrations, their conclusions that nobody cares about their immediate plights and their futures. They are the losers in a changing world, and they know and resent it.

In recent years I've been fortunate to spend hours in the company of H. L. Hix and enjoy his friendship. In all that time I've never seen him angry. In fact, he's usually amused and bemused, happily carrying someone's baby in his arms, brilliant when giving a talk or reading his poems and reciting those of others from memory. *American Anger* demonstrates his profound capacity to empathize with people whose lives are so different from his own. I consider this collection important because it speaks so well, and through poetry, to a matter than has become so central in American culture and politics. "Behind every great man there's a fury. Better chafed than sorry," Hix writes.

> Better the pistol you know than the pistol you don't
> Better hate than anger.
>
> — "Aggression Cue 2: A hand slammed on a table"

Although the book's title and the poems throughout use and reuse the word "anger," Hix implies that "hate" and "fury" are more appropriate words for the state of mind of the millions and for their need to strike out at all those they blame for their unhappy conditions. The American Psychological Association describes a continuum of anger, from the acceptable to the extreme:

> Anger is a completely normal, usually healthy, human emotion. But when it gets out of control and turns destructive, it can lead to problems—problems at work, in your personal relationships, and in the overall quality of your life. And it can make you feel as though you're at the mercy of an unpredictable and powerful emotion.

In "Compromised Sonnet: Compromising Rationalization," Hix writes:

> A violent man, like a ministry of defense,
> will justify his violence with some version of
> *I had to. I was provoked beyond endurance.*

(Note that the italics in this passage and others quoted appeared in the originals.)

Hix's poems penetrate the mentality of the out-of-control, capturing the idiom of the furious, but also contemplating the nature of anger through the theories of philosophers and psychologists. He, too, relates individual anger to national militaristic anger, the justifications behind wars.

> How may we aptly designate the discrepancy between
> Our claim to collective sainthood—"one nation under
>   god"—
> and our assignment of others to an "axis of evil"?
> By calling it *American anger.*
>
> "Preamble: Nomination Anthem"

Rather than attempting to explain American anger, Hix illustrates and often dramatizes its multiple manifestations. He does cite the theories of others directly and indirectly, as evidenced in an 18-page listing of works cited, such as books by Barbara Ehrenreich, Richard Hofstadter, and Martha Nussbaum, though many other authors whose names are new to me. Ultimately, Hix sees anger as a complex set of reactions and behaviors arising from a wide set of circumstances, as in:

> But what you're describing is fear. People lash out
>     when they're afraid.
> Groups lash out when group members perceive
>     the group or themselves
> as threatened. (And this perception need not be
>     acknowledged: a white
> supremacist's unwillingness to admit feeling
>     threatened by blacks
> doesn't mean he doesn't feel threatened.) Yes, of
>     course,
> anger is fear. But no more than it is violence,
> greed, lust, despair, hatred, prejudice, need,
>     ignorance,
> victimization, hunger, helplessness, hopelessness,
>     aggressions.
> You're saying fear might cause anger,
> and it might be assuaged by it;
> I'm saying anger is subsumed by fear, is but
> One aspect or manifestation of it.
>
> "Anger related to fear:"

While the collection offers multiple variations on a theme, the poems—divided into eight discrete sections—are far from redundant, instead rich in their inventiveness, their variations of rhetoric, their ironic connections, their rhythmic catalogues, but ultimately in the perceptiveness of their insights.

One of Hix's most profound insights is found in the collection's section titled "Erinyeneutics," a compound word that Hix created. He is linking hermeneutics and fury by

substituting for the messenger god Hermes the Erinyes—
also known as the Furies, the goddesses of vengeance. The
poems in this section serve as commentaries on and reversals of the Furies' exhortations. The great majority are Hix's
translations of, primarily, ancient Greek poems, along with
a few Roman, French, and Spanish poems. They exhort
readers to control anger, with lines such as:

> Outrage, nurtured to full ripeness, bears
> a crop of folly and a harvest of tears
> Yield your anger, permit yourself change.
> You would rebut your rage, if you understood.
> Like bodies seen through fog, faults seen through
> anger look larger. Let one who
> is hungry have food, but let one who would chas-
> tise have for it no hunger of thirst.

(Note that the sources are not identified until the book's
final pages, in a separate listing called "Attributions." The
lines are from text by Aeschylus, Sophocles, Euripides, Plato,
and others. The titles given the full excerpts are Hix's.)

Unfortunately, the wisdom of the ancient Greeks has
been lost on many who are now themselves lost in the
raging passions of American anger. Imagine what would
happen to someone who stood up and quoted these lines
at certain political rallies. The rallying are seething with
despair at their social impotence because their lives and
work have counted for nothing, while others have gotten
so rich. More and more, social and political commentators
admit that these people are justified in their realizations
that they have been left out and left behind. The system
must find ways to address their lives and their legitimate
needs. If nothing is done to alleviate their dilemmas, the
danger is a social explosion.

Hix portrays a number of scenarios of the potential outcomes in the final section of the collection, "Lost Wax." He does this though a series of invented narratives exemplifying human rage. The book's final poem, "What is it to be overcome with anger?" relates the memory of a fictional first-person narrator. He was in the third grade, and his father took him to a minor-league baseball game. The boy had to pee, but, unfamiliar with a stadium's men's room, walked past the line of waiting men straight to the urinal. A man in a tie and jacket, smiling, tapped his shoulder to tell him about the protocol of the line. The boy's father went wild, "Don't you / fuckin ever fuckin touch my fuckin son." Then he beat the man, punching him again and again until pulled off by others. When someone says, "cop," the boy's father grabs his son and runs to his car, speeding away. As the son starts crying, the father backhands the boy's nose with a knuckle and makes it bleed. "Men don't cry," he says, "and men don't let themselves get pushed around." His final words before the silent drive home are, "Time you learn to fight back." That's American anger, the Furies unleashed.

An immediate reaction to this poem might be condemnation of the father, a man capable of beating a stranger for an imagined slight to his son, in large measure because that man is of a status that allows him to wear a tie and jacket, implying that the father resents his own lower social and economic class. "I've got a family to defend." Yet, rather than excusing the father, it's possible to understand him and perhaps even view him with a form of empathy. Yes, lock him up, but also give him help.

*American Anger* is both disturbing and illuminating. It's doubtful that those who manifest the anger will buy or read Hix's poems. Those of us who do should realize that we are not looking at a freak show but rather at people in pain.

**Works Cited:**
American Psychological Association, "Controlling anger before it controls you." blogpost consulted October 2016.
Hix, H.L. *American Anger: An Evidentiary*. Etruscan Press, 2016.

# *The Invertiscope: Multiple Realities in* Mount Terminus

*When I had an invitation to write a review of David Grand's* Mount Terminus, *the purpose called for a stance of seeming objective analysis. A personal essay would have been inappropriate. That meant I couldn't explain I've known David as a friend and colleague for more than a decade or that I've experienced readings of his various approaches to the material for the novel throughout the eleven years of its writing. Nor could I refer to our conversations about his creative dilemmas. I recall that the very first opening version I heard (perhaps there had been earlier) involved a cataclysmic fire at a Hollywood movie studio in the early years of motion pictures. He was not satisfied, in part because of what he considered the constraint of writing about a real place. His first two novels,* Louse *and* The Disappearing Body, *are set in imaginary locations. Though the resulting final version of* Mount Terminus *(which had the tentative title of* Rosenbloom *for years) does involve considerable research in the early history of Los Angeles, the movie industry, and the optical technology behind movie cameras, I believe the invention of the title local,* Mount Terminus, *gave David the assurance of a made-up setting to embody and transform the integration of necessary factual details. But beyond the place, the characters, and the events, what may be most impressive about the novel is its narrative voice. Or it just may be that as I read words on the page they came alive with the sound of David's rhythms and resonances.*

Among the many invented optical devices crucial to David Grand's novel, *Mount Terminus*, the invertiscope is the most fascinating, an essential commentary on the way people apprehend the world around them. For this novel is about the creation of worlds—constructed places, fabricated realities of art and film, realms of mystery, tangles of memory, and spheres of imagination.

Experiencing the invertiscope teaches the central character, Joseph Rosenblum (referred to as Bloom throughout), that what the human eye takes in is inadequate, limited in perspective and missing the fullness of possibilities. Invented by Isabella, Bloom's first love, the device is shaped like the shaft of a periscope, with a number of angled mirrors that can be manipulated by pulleys. The result is a greatly expanded field of vision that is transformative rather than merely ocular. For Bloom it is like stepping out of his own skin, released "from his containment to become an invisible interloper looking down on his own life." He learns "that perception isn't absolute, that the mind and body are capable of adapting to new associations."

Bloom's perceptual adaptations make *Mount Terminus* a unique *bildungsroman*. Like other protagonists of that form, Bloom does endure a series of trying experiences to achieve moral and psychological development. He is, however, enveloped by fabulous circumstances, a world alive with allusions to history, myth, fairy tales, and Biblical stories, yet unique in itself. The novel contains good and evil twins, long separated siblings, lush gardens and wastelands, helpers and villains, monsters and visions of beauty, and ultimately a paradisiacal island. Like Bloom envisioning with new perceptions and associations, David

Grand transforms familiar tropes into a unique reality, distinct settings and gatherings of human dramas made richer through their echoes of ancient stories melded into the landscape of California and the history of Los Angeles and the film industry. As if seeing through an invertiscope, Grand manipulates the pulleys, but does it seamlessly, without exposing his creative hands at work.

The opposite faces of the Mount Terminus's reality are revealed by the panorama Bloom views the first time his father, Jacob, brings him up the heights to their villa, the father's retreat, an estate high above and apart from the world below:

> For as far as he could see, there was emptiness. No homes. No people. No vestiges of civilization past or present. When they reached a series of escalating plateaus stepping up to the mountain's peak, they stopped at a blackened gate, beyond which was land so bright with color, in these barren wastes it seemed implausible it should exist.

A place of such color could be an Edenic refuge from the wasteland. But the setting is already corrupted by prior events that undermine its possibilities as a refuge. Once father and son pass through the gate and arrive at the villa, Bloom is taken for a walk about the grounds, where he experiences "an empty field," "a sickly odor," "land aswirl in dust," "a deep ravine," "violet sediment on the horizon."

Although Bloom, once removed to the mountain, never leaves during his boyhood and youth and into the cusp of adulthood, his life is enveloped by the past and present of the world outside, first as ominous unknowns he is driven to explore and later as an accumulation of bewildering and disturbing information. His isolation and innocence make him especially vulnerable to threats beyond his comprehension.

Throughout, Bloom is bewildered by people and their motives. In the spirit of the invertiscope, seeing himself and his experiences as if looking down at them, he needs a perspective that permits him to give substance and meaning to his own life.

Mystery upon mystery envelopes Bloom—what happened to his mother; his father's bleak silence; his mother's enigmatic drawings; the recurrence of the men in black coats; a series of puzzling notes slipped to him by the mute housekeeper, Roya; her guidance though dark passages to Manuel Salazar's secret chamber; a document in Spanish; and, throughout, the shocks of additional revelations.

Bloom craves a means of vision that will allow him to make sense of this bombardment. It is the movie camera, a technological parallel to the invertiscope, that becomes the means through which Bloom eventually uses to replicate and grasp events that have distressed him, as another way of looking down at his own life. Bloom's father's, Jacob's, fortune came from his invention of a device, the Rosenbloom Loop, capable of projecting continuous reels of film and producing larger than life images. Movies, that modern form of mythmaking, are inseparable from the myths of Bloom's existence and his inevitable outlet to give those myths tangible form.

*Death, Forlorn,* the small book his father carried with him everywhere, and which Jacob asks Bloom to illustrate, becomes the source of the son's first real film achievement. The orphaned Bloom then emulates his father by continually carrying the book in his own pocket. To truly achieve his film, his directorial mentor, Gottlieb, demands that

Bloom understand what it means to be deeply in love, "the visceral upheaval only a tormented heart can provide." Yet, at this stage of his life, Bloom has never known such love, the kind of love that has ruined his parents' lives. He must experience this suffering before he can create.

When *Death, Forlorn* is completed, Isabella, his companion in filmmaking, disappears, leaving a note that explains little, yet another mystery. In his grief, he decides to create one final picture for Isabella: *The Death of Paradise*, the tormented tale of Miranda, a former resident of Mount Terminus; her brutal husband, Don Fernando Miguel Estrella; her sensual maid, Adora; and her secret lover, Manuel Salazar, Fernando's cousin. It's a tale of love, abuse, self-poisoning, imprisonment, defilement, and vicious murders, much more sensational and violent than the events that ruined Bloom's parents, yet still essential to the grim heritage of Mount Terminus. A peep hole figures prominently in Salazar's ability to observe so much from his hidden chamber, just as a camera lens functions as an observant eye to capture action on film, and as the invertiscope reveals unknowns.

As Salazar's story is exposed, Bloom learns of source of his home's name. Banished to the California territory by the king of Spain, Fernando called his estate Mount Terminus because he considered the site of his exile "the end of the world," the role it later takes on for Jacob, the role it threatens for Bloom.

Late in the novel, when a dam breaks and a wall of water "devour[s] all of what stood fixed on the landscape," Bloom, trapped in his car, expects Death's approach, but he experiences only a mist like "the kiss of life." In what he believed would be his last moments, he imagines a future on an island he had visited, remembering "how blissful and at peace he had been there." Such an island may be the mirrored obverse of Mount Terminus, demonstrating the lesson of the invertiscope "that the mind and body are capable of adapting to new associations."

Beyond its many pleasures of story and invention, David Grand's *Mount Terminus* can be considered a master class in how to create a unique novelistic world. Grand achieves a flawless integration of mythic sources with the actual landscape of Southern California and the history of the movie industry, but most of all with a rich complexity of human lives. Grand's recreations transfigure myths, landscapes, and histories into an original reality unlike any other.

# The Worlds of the Ordinary: Chris Arthur's On the Shoreline of Knowledge: Irish Wanderings

*While Chris Arthur and I have been in contact for a number of years, the great majority of those exchanges have been via email. I met him in person only once when he was a visiting writing at one of our MFA residencies at Wroxton College in England. My introduction to Chris was an essay he submitted to* The Literary Review *during the period I was the quarterly's editor. At first reading, I knew his work was special, unique in its depth of contemplation and the surprising shifts of illumination. It was a pleasure to follow the brilliance of his imagination. The review that follows, like that of David Grand's* Mount Terminus, *does not refer to our friendship; but I hope my fondness for Chris and his work emerges.*

Unique among writers of personal essays, Chris Arthur, in this new collection, as in his previous books, does not seek insights into himself or words that convey the essential drama of his life. Instead, the knowledge he pursues is a deeper understanding of his quotidian experiences—a chestnut found in a coat pocket, a list of mammals he compiled at age five, a pencil taken from the ground near a school, a photo of a boy with his first bicycle—in the much greater context of the natural, historical, philosophical, and spiritual; in short, how the smallest and seemingly insignificant detail relates to the totality. In this sense, what happened to Arthur, distinct happenings, do not function as access into the man himself, but rather as representative of all our lives, starting points for exploring the connections of the personal with the world around us. What Arthur does reveal is his intellect, the workings of his subtle and curious mind, not his psyche.

In the essay "Lists" he writes: "The desire to order things, to find palatable interpretations of the world, is at the heart of much of our endeavor. We are a pattern-seeking species hungry for the articulation of experiences into sense and for those shapes of intelligibility by which the brute face of being may be tamed into person-centered scales. We need to extract some kind of navigable meaning for life's gargantuan liquid flow, which, without our efforts to dam and irrigate it, would sweep us away in a tidal wave of incomprehension. Language is our primary tool in this."

These essays could be considered exemplars of Blake's world in a grain of sand, "the depth of meaning contained in the seeming shallows of the ordinary." But in this case objects Arthur has encountered throughout his life do not yield their vastness from within. The grain opens up worlds of complex relationships through introspection, speculation, and research. In this approach Arthur can be considered an interdisciplinary writer, integrating the findings of extensive reading and historical associations with the musings of his own imagination to provide evidence that supports his contemplations.

Arthur's title for this collection, *Shoreline of Knowledge*, suggests the geography of his home nation, the island of Ireland, surrounded by the sea, and Arthur often writes of water and coastlines. Yet he transcends that literal sea by suggesting the expanse that encompasses the particulars of our singular lives and locations, and the need to plunge in from the shores of our selves to seek a greater knowledge.

His subtitle, *Irish Wanderings*, may imply a travelogue of journeys throughout that landscape. The word Irish may be found in the titles of almost all Arthur's books. But he is not just a literal traveler through a physical landscape. Northern Ireland is his birthplace, the home of his youth, though he spent many of adult years in Wales and now lives in Scotland. A memory from that time in Ireland functions as a starting point for his writing, with the actual wanderings taking Arthur in many directions as his mind navigates a labyrinth of information, references, and possibilities.

For Arthur ordinary places "exert an authority on the psyche." But why? What is their power over us? Each identifies the mystery of a specific ordinary, and he functions as a sleuth attempting to solve that mystery. Unlike the protagonists of detective fiction who comfort readers with the certainty of their resolutions, Arthur frames possibilities instead of absolutes. The answer could be this or it could be that or even something else. We live in the midst of unknowns and weave stories to confront them: "So we clutch at the things around us, put them in our pockets when we can, take what comfort there is to be found in them, salvage what shreds of sense appear in the entangled savagery and sweetness of life's unfolding."

Arthur emphasizes contingencies, "the proximity of other outcomes ... how 'otherwise' is our constant companion." Writing of the "miracle" of his uncle's survival amid a fusillade of gunfire during World War Two, he says, "So many things seem as if, so easily, they might never have happened. Seemingly trivial events carry gargantuan implications."

Arthur's method of pursuing those implications is circular, each essay a compilation of smaller essays that return to the initial "trivial" event or object and consider it from a different perspective. In his introduction to the collection, "Going Around in Circles," he explains his reliance on the Zen concept of *ensō*, going round in circles, a concept "variously taken to represent enlightenment, clear seeing, the absolute, one-pointedness of concentration, the universe," suggesting that this approach yields more epiphanies than a straight path.

The essay "Thirteen Ways of Looking at a Briefcase," a homage to the Stevens' blackbird poem, is one demonstration of Arthur's approach. It begins with the image of a herd of calves among the hillocks of Ireland's County Down, narrowing in to the particular calf whose flesh became this briefcase. The next section is the opposite of idyllic, conjuring the horrors of the slaughterhouse with death, skinning, and tanning, a reminder of how animals are transformed into leather objects. Then it strikes him that the briefcase in question could have come from many parts of the world, not just Ireland. Arthur realizes "The briefcase, which on its own seems so limited, straightforward, closed—uninteresting—in fact harbors unexpected doors, locked only by our strange custom of not trying them; doors that give access to other times, other places, that quickly lead from the ordinary into the extraordinary."

Yet the next section returns to the mundane, an almost technical description of the briefcase—its color, shape, texture, its signs of use. Then Arthur tells the reader that though a stranger might see the briefcase as a trivial object, to him it sings as sweetly as a blackbird. The sixth section reveals the briefcase was his father's, the source of a flood of memories, a trigger point opening "another dimension."

Part of that dimension is the role the briefcase played in his father's career in Northern Ireland's Ministry of Finance, holding the government papers he carried back and forth on his daily commute from their home village to Belfast. This fact leads to a consideration of the politics of the time and the likelihood that, unaware to his apolitical father, those papers may have played a role in the suppression of Catholics by the Protestant majority, a condition that led to violence and many deaths.

Still, it was Arthur's father's briefcase, suggesting a "skin-to-skin" communion when touched by the son years after his parent's death. The complexity of its associations makes Arthur think of the Book of Kells he once saw with his father in Trinity College Dublin's Old Library, and beyond that an exhibit of one hundred objects presented by Neil MacGregor, a director of the British Museum, who said, "Telling history through *things* is what museums are for." Although the father's briefcase would not have been one of those objects, like them it connects "with the personal and the planetary, with lineages of individuals and species."

Finally, Arthur considers what may be held in common between multiple ways of looking at a briefcase and looking at a blackbird, and he remembers the blackbird is Ireland's totemic bird, evoking a childhood memory of seeking blackbird nests in "secret, hidden bowers," his father, when Arthur was very small, lifting him to see the eggs: "Sometimes I think of the briefcase now as a kind of nest crammed with a treasure trove of eggs."

Once again, in this essay, as in those of the entire collection and in all Arthur's writing, an object from his life and its associated personal memories lead to ruminations that demonstrate the web of relationships binding the specifics of an individual life to patterns of history, to natural processes, to ideas, and to the endless connections that animate the world around us, past and present. Although, in circling around its subjects, Arthur essays follow a similar approach, they transcend redundancy because each set of discoveries offers a new range of surprising illuminations.

# *Christopher Meredith,* The Book of Idiots

*Like my relationship with Chris Arthur, mine with Christopher Meredith originated through my association with* The Literary Review. *He was—with Tony Curtis—the co-editor of an issue devoted to contemporary Welsh writing, of which he is an important representative as poet, novelist, and translator. Our in-person meeting occurred when he and his wife, Val, traveled to Manhattan for a reading launch of the issue. (The issue came out not long after my wife and I had spent a week the Yorkshire Dales village of West Burton, staying in a flat in a converted mill just steps from a waterfall. My conversation with Val revealed that they had stayed in the same mill, if not the same flat, a year before. What are the odds?) I didn't hear from Christopher for a number of years after than, not until he sent me the novel discussed in this review. As a result, I was able to get him to write two essays for the website* The Literary Explorer, *about his experiences as a writing fellow in Finland and in Slovenia. He tells of responding to a request to speak Welsh and having the Slovenes cry out, "Oh my God! It's Elvish!"*

The title of Welsh writer Christopher Meredith's fourth novel, *The Book of Idiots*, may remind some of the various instructional guides for mastering everything from chess to beekeeping. In this case, the characters demonstrate how to make a hash out of your life. They are idiots in the sense that we all are. To paraphrase Flaubert, "Un idiot, c'est moi." Or Walt Kelly's Pogo, "I have met the idiots and it is us." Meredith's characters—Clive, Wil, Matt, Jeff, and others, as well as the narrator, Dean Lloyd—all do idiotic things and cringe at their follies. When Matt calls Dean clever, Dean responds, "Just differently idiotic."

It's also a novel about dying. In the opening chapter Dean recalls a kids' game called Best Man's Fall. The one designated On It has an imaginary gun to shoot and kill all the others. The point was, having been shot, performing an act of aesthetic, artistic, athletic, and authentic dying. The one chosen the best became the next On It. But none of the kids considered that a reward. Much more important was the chance to demonstrate the art of dying. Several of the adults, no longer playing a game, do die in the following chapters, but while authentically dead, haven't made their demise a work of art. First, you idiotically fail at living, and then you die.

While one reviewer in the UK calls the novel a "hilarious black comedy," I found it much more sad than funny. While the characters often make fools of themselves, to laugh at them requires a distancing. Here, although Dean seems to maintain a removal from some of the people he tells about, for example, avoiding a post-swim beer with Jeff, even in his reticence he reveals a compassionate connection. As noted, he is aware that he is just a different kind of idiot.

In fact, the novel does not disclose much about Dean's circumstances. He has an unspecified tedious job in a mundane office. He meets others, especially his friend Wil, and listens to their stories, though saying almost nothing about himself to them. He seems to want to avoid complications, in one case doing a U-turn when a serious accident happens ahead of him on a crowded highway, in another leaving a seriously injured man once he is assured an ambulance is on its way. Dean does have an unnamed wife and family and goes to Crete on vacation. But at points throughout the telling of the novel it's revealed that he is speaking to a "you" whom he is eager to meet and who has been in his car with him. By all implications, this you is a lover, but not identified as explicitly as those of other men in the novel. Marriages are inadequate. They do not make people happy, but neither do affairs.

Several stories run through the novel, mainly that of Wil, less so those of Matt, Clive, and Jeff. Chapters about them alternate with the facts of Dean's work and drives, accumulating details as they fill in and surprise. By far the most compelling is Wil's tale of accidentally meeting a lover from his youth in a hospital waiting room and the drama of what happens next; it runs though much of the novel, building a suspenseful tension.

Acutely aware of life's messiness and human inadequacies, Dean yearns for a perfection that would achieve the vanishing of self. He reveals it when telling of his never-realized goal in a swimming pool: "But the aim is to smooth that [lengths of the pool] out and make it one unfaltering line at one speed. ...The result should be a kind of emptiness if you were ever to achieve the perfect line. You'd collapse into the line of your own movement and become a point." On the final page of the novel, above the earth in a glider and not sure where he is, Dean is told by Peter, the plane's pilot, "Hardest thing in the world. ... Flying in a straight line." Much easier to act like an idiot.

For all his struggles with being, Dean observes with

great precision, which is, of course, a reflection of Meredith's ability with description and with the rendering of complexities, such as the unfaltering line. An author of four poetry collections, Meredith is also a master of dialogue, capturing distinctive speech patterns that reveal the essence of the people behind them.

*The Book of Idiots* impresses at many levels—structure, language, characterization, and insights. Unfortunately, released by Seren Books, an imprint of Poetry Wales, it does not yet have an American publisher. Fortunately, the novel is available though Amazon.co.uk and deserves the widest possible readership.

# *Greg Herriges,* JD: A Memoir of a Time and a Journey

*I wrote this review before Greg Herriges and I became friends and I produced three of his books—a story collection and two novels—as the then co-publisher of Serving House Books. I admire them as much as I do JD. But at the time of this review I had no personal information about the man beyond what he offers in this work itself. Still, what he offers is considerable given the personal nature of the quest he describes.*

It's no mystery why there is such a mystique around J.D. Salinger. More than forty years ago, at the peak of a fame other writers could barely fantasize, he stopped publishing and became a recluse. Yet where he lives [*JD* was published before Salinger's death] is no secret—a house in Cornish, New Hampshire. But he's inaccessible, at least to anyone who wants to probe his personal life and the state of his writing career. Getting an interview with Salinger would be a literary equivalent of finding the Holy Grail or the remains of Jimmy Hoffa. Yet Greg Herriges pulled it off. That was almost thirty years ago, and the appearance of his article about the experience in a magazine called *Oui* began his publishing career, which includes stories, three novels, and now the complete tale of his quest for Salinger.

Herriges first revealed "the story behind the story" to T.C. Boyle in a hotel bar, who advised him to turn the material into a short story or a novel. Although Boyle "lit the fire," Herriges decided to tell what happened directly. "Fiction," he says, "would have been the wrong venue." In the end, the technicality of genre doesn't matter. Though called a memoir, *JD* reads like a novel, compelling from one page to the next, filled with people and events that seem like the products of an inspired imagination but resonate even more because they are grounded in authenticity.

While Salinger does appear for a few minutes in the driveway outside the garage of a house that has no other entrance, this work is not really about him. Herriges himself become the main character, and the unintended quest turns out to be a search for himself, the famous man just a catalyst for the journey.

That's not to say Salinger was incidental to his life, merely a journalistic coup. Reaching Salinger in Cornish was equivalent to finding the sage on the mountaintop, the source of a meaning that had at a crucial time grounded Herriges' fragile existence. In the midst of a "hellish adolescence" and a dysfunctional, absent-father family, Herriges "went interior. I lost myself in a world or rock and roll and literature." The greatest impact came from a chance discovery of *The Catcher in the Rye*, a novel that mesmerized him from the first page on: "The power of Salinger's writing stunned me, lifted me up when I most needed lifting, and presented a resplendent new way of looking at the world. I was hooked. I wanted more."

At age 27, teaching tough kids in an inner-city Chicago high school, Herriges hoped *Catcher* would do for his students what it had done for him. Instead, his students kept asking why Salinger didn't write anymore, speculating that he had enough money not to, Herriges losing it and yelling at the student who suggested Salinger was just burned out.

It's clear that one of Herriges' motives for the quest was proving to himself that a man so vital to his own identity as a person and to his own goal of becoming a writer was still engaged in his art, still a creative presence despite his absence from the printed page.

But *JD* is not just a tale about Herriges and Salinger. A third character enters the book early on and in many ways overwhelms it, just as she, Sarah—a teacher who comes to his school—overwhelms Herriges: "Warm eyes, olive skin—a counterculture Fanny Glass, then, if you will. She radiated. There was virtual fallout form her bohemian aura when she walked by." If she had been pure invention, Sarah would be up there with the most tempting of femmes fatale, la belle dames sans merci. And Sarah doesn't come alone. Lurking in the background till the final chapters is Dan, Herriges' rival, the source of Sarah's mood swings.

At her insistence, Sarah (not her real name) does not appear in the 1978 article about the visit to Salinger. But she exists at the heart of this book, the most dominant of the many quests *JD* depicts. Ultimately, this is a tale of obsessions—finding Salinger, winning Sarah, becoming a writer, coming to terms with an abandoning father, discovering one's identity.

It's no mystery that Herriges encountered Salinger and succeeded as a writer. We know those answers from the early pages and from the author's biography. But the fate of the love affair and Herriges' life for the past three decades remain unknowns until the final pages. Beyond the vividness with which Herriges conveys the surface adventures, *JD* is much more than a celebrity hunt. The book's profound human complexities give it emotional depth.

# *Duff Brenna,* The Willow Man

*Duff and I are long-time friends, even serving as each oth-er's editor and publisher. But this is the only one of his many books I've written about. Fortunately, he's won awards and much praise without my input. He deserves even more.*

Like Huck Finn, Duff Brenna's Triple E—Elbert Earl Evans—lights out for the territory ahead, and he's done it in two novels, first *Too Cool* (1998) and now *The Willow Man*. With each flight he travels farther and far-ther from civilization, deeper and deeper into a physical and a psychic wilderness. Unlike Huck, whose journey on the Mississippi River never strays far from the communi-ties on either bank, and who is an innocent initiated into knowledge of the follies, treacheries, and hypocrisies of the society around him, Triple E at seventeen is already hardened, a juvenile delinquent just out of reform school, cynical and violent, abiding by no laws.

In *The Willow Man*'s powerful opening he sets out to rob an evil old man called John Brown, and beat him to a pulp "just to be mean," but ends up being pummeled to near death and thrown off the back of a pickup truck into black water. Brown becomes his nemesis and his quest. Not only has he humiliated Triple E physically, he has abducted the young girl, Mercy Justice Jones, Triple E has vowed to protect and comes to love despite himself. In his delusion, Brown believes she is his long-gone daughter and calls her by that name, Mamie. (The full Brown-Mamie story was the subject of Brenna's 1990 novel, *The Book of Mamie*.) From then on the forward action of the novel becomes a manhunt, Triple E plunging into an icy Alaskan no man's land, tested to track his prey and, even more significantly, to survive.

The other half of the novel, in alternating chapters, tells how Triple E violated parole and got from Minnesota to Alaska, how he started out with a friend in the souped-up car they engineered and came to meet Mercy and her mother, how he abandoned his friend Lee, how he and Mercy ended up in Whitehorse, Alaska, she singing her own songs in a local bar for tips, how John Brown came into their lives.

Brenna succeeds with two main challenges in *The Willow Man*. He has to make the reader empathize with Triple E despite his criminality, his violent outbursts, his destructiveness, his hardened hostilities. We accept because, as much as he resists it, Triple E reveals a search for meaning, some value in the tooth and claw world around him. And we accept, perhaps grudgingly, because of his toughness, his willingness to start a fight and kill men worse than he is. Brenna avoids the sentimentality of portraying Triple E's criminality as merely a veneer over an essentially good heart. His destructiveness seems rooted in hopelessness, a welcoming of extreme risk because death doesn't matter. As much as he needs to save Mercy's, Triple E has to save his own life.

But beyond his achievement in creating such a character, Brenna gives the Alaskan landscape an overwhelming presence in the novel, not just a setting for Triple E's adventures, instead a living presence that embodies all he must overcome—environment, people, self. And Brenna does this through the power of his writing, his physical descriptions:

... Looking over the side, he sees a thousand feet of sheerness. The cliff curves in at the bottom, like a narrow waist. There is no way he can climb down it. The only way out is up. He is appalled at his bad luck. He sits on a rock, closes his eyes. Tries to think. He puts his mitten over his fact to shield it from the wind. Always the wind. Everywhere the wind alive and hating him, insulting him. It sucks away his breath, tears at his face, all the while shrilly screaming.

Far more than an adventure story, *The Willow Man* rises to the level of a mythic confrontation—man struggling with nature, with an enemy who is the Other, and with the inward forces that tear at his being.

# Reviews of Three Novels by Linda Lappin

*Linda Lappin is the only one of the friends in this collection whose books I've written about but who I've never actually met, though I know several people who have shared time with her in Europe at various writers' workshop and residencies. She and I did have one brief transatlantic phone conversation, both surprised that our voices were not what we expected after many email exchanges. It's been a pleasure to know her virtually and to have the opportunity to read and write about some of her books.*

## The Etruscan

Among the pleasures of *The Etruscan* are a compelling plot, a group of intriguing characters, a vivid sense of place, and strong descriptive writing. But Linda Lappin's principal achievement—and greatest challenge—may be found in her realization of Count Frederigo Del Re and the strange power he exerts over the novel's heroine, Harriet Sackett.  Del Re, who claims Etruscan ancestry, embodies the title. Closely examining a stone-carved mask, Stephen Hampton, Harriet's skeptical cousin, thinks:

> It was some sort of propitiatory god...a spirit of the woods or waters, and, from the looks of it, was a genuine piece of antiquity, although he found it an ugly thing, with a mockingly perverse expression. He did not care for Etruscan arts in general.

The Etruscans were a vicious and cruel people ...

Although Hampton believes Del Re "was only a phantom of Harriet's overwrought" imagination, the reader knows this emotional reaction reveals how a man of his background and sensibility would have reacted to Del Re's appearance. But Harriet, both fascinated and repelled, is overpowered. Early in their relationship, stunned by the sensation of Del Re's presence, she has a realization: "I knew I would come to love the owner of that hand with a desperation I never imagined possible, yet all the same I felt a foretaste of revulsion."

Lappin's task—or that of any writer who wishes to create a Frederigo Del Re—is convincing the reader to share Harriet's complex, almost otherworldly, obsession with the man. In *The Etruscan* she succeeds.

From the title alone, one might expect a novel set in the distant past, a pre-*Aeneid* setting. The work is, in fact, historical but placed in a much more recent time, the 1920s and ending in 1945. It begins in London in the Russell Square home of Stephen and Sarah Hampton, but quickly moves to Italy and the area around the village of Vitorchiano in Tuscia, site of the Etruscan relics that Harriet has gone to photograph. Lappin knows both the time period and the geography well. She has been writing a series of essays on women writers and artists of the Twenties, and she has lived in Italy since 1978.

Stephen Hampton and Wimbly are men in their fifties, Sarah and Harriet women of about forty. Harriet is Stephen's American-educated cousin, whose mother had run off with a no-account American; Sarah is her American-born school friend with whom Stephen fell in love.

Wimbly, a widower back from India, would like to marry Harriet; but she is a bohemian who travels about the world with a camera and wearing trousers instead of ladylike dresses. Her project this time is Etruscan ruins. When the Hamptons do not hear from her for a long period, they send Mrs Parsons to Italy. The housekeeper discovers a desperately ill Harriet and the first part of her diary. With that the intrigue begins.

While the novel has a twenty-first century publication date and a twentieth-century setting, many of its narrative strategies are Victorian, with the Gothic overtones found in writers like the Brontës. Del Re is clearly a Byronic figure in the tradition of Rochester and Heathcliffe. Mystery lies at the heart of the story—for much of the novel the question of what happened to Harriet in Italy and, even after the final page, the nature of what draws her to Del Re. In addition to the overt unknowns, several surprises come as shocks— what once happened between Stephen and Harriet, Del Re's real background, the lost decades of Harriet's life. Yet, once revealed, the reader realizes they have been prepared for.

Two realities are contrasted, that of Edwardian per-spectives of Wimbly, the Hamptons, and the Hampton's housekeeper, Mrs Parsons, and that of Harriet's immer-sion in another realm. Lappin presents the attitudes and perceptions of Wimbly, the Hamptons, and Mrs Parsons in close third person. But Harriet emerges directly through her first-person diary, a document like that found in many traditional novels. The physical diary itself becomes an object of contention, with Stephen trying to burn it, Mrs Parsons rescuing it, and Sarah preserving the final, torn out page until its content is revealed on the very last pages of the novel.

The Italian settings are certainly Gothic, the ancient homes, the treacherous landscapes, the Etruscan tombs. Because of Lappin's exact descriptions, they are very convincing:

> Off the cloister a small chapel stood intact. The iron gate creaked as he pushed it open and we stepped inside. The warped wooden pews were coated with dust. Snail shells had collected at the base of the altar, a swallow's nest hung from the rafters. We walked down the aisle and stopped before the altar where a shriveled bouquet of wild flowers lay amid brown rose petals and the withered bodies of dead bees. ...

Of even greater importance for the novel's fulfillment is the need for the reader to grasp Del Re. Lappin provides the same precision of detail:

> Federigo Del Re seemed older in the scrutiny of sunlight. A stubble of white beard sprouted on his chin where the skin beneath was no longer firm and taut, and yet hardly a wrinkle was etched in his face. His features were an odd composite of contrasts: the thin lips of an aesthete, the jutting forehead of a brooder, the full cheeks of a sensualist. With his eyes closed, the energy and light had drained away from him. He looked grey and sad, quite different from the bronze masks blazing in the lamplight that I had glimpsed earlier in the tomb. This unexpected vulnerability in him moved me and I reached out hesitantly to touch his face....

For Harriet, "I had never felt so drawn to any man or woman." That's the essence of the novel.

## *Signatures in Stone*

Linda Lappin's compelling novel offers a Chinese box of mysteries, one inside another and all parts of a larger whole. Each box is pried open as the story drives toward its resolution. But the question is, will one box become more crucial than the others, exposing unexpected answers that rearrange all our assumptions? Will certain characters be revealed as existing in an external box that hides the internal? It's to Lappin's great credit that she creates such an intriguing and substantial world.

Set in the 1920s in a reimagining of what had been a historical Italian province called Tuscia, an area much more primitive in landscape and beliefs than, say, the supposedly nearby Tuscany, the tale is told by a woman-of-a-certain-age (her term for herself) mystery novelist named Daphne DuBlanc. Born and raised on an English estate that was driven into debt by her late improvident brother, and now widowed, penniless, and drug-dependent, Daphne finds herself in a remote and dilapidated Italian villa rented by her publisher, Nigel, ordered to write another of the mystery novels that have become her means of support, meager as that support is. With her are the homosexual Nigel; a handsome but seemingly talentless Texan painter named Clive; a young Roman called Danilo; American Professor Finestone, from whom Nigel has rented a section of the villa; the unkempt Manu, who acts as a handyman; Manu's strange apparent daughter, Amelia, sadly wanting as a cook and cleaner but alluring to several of the males; and Amelia's scrawny, rheumy-eyed white cat. So we have a mystery writer trying to create a new work in the midst of a group of enigmatic people living on an estate adjacent to an overgrown park of hellish Renaissance sculptures called the Sacred Wood. At first the gate to the wood is locked, but once opened, it gives an entry to a foreboding and treacherous landscape.

While the people and the unpredictable actions around them are sources of unknowns, at least from the perspective of Daphne, who often finds herself threatened and disoriented, the villa itself, lit only by candlelight, is a place of many shadows, hidden passageways, strange noises, crumbling walls, and rare art of great worth. People and forces can emerge from the darkness or literally drop out of the ceiling.

The Sacred Wood exists as an overt mystery, subject of a monograph Professor Finestone says he is writing on his clacking typewriter. He hints at the role of a major Renaissance artist in the creation of the wood, claiming his findings will lead to a revolution in art history, but offering nothing of his work's content. The sculptures have to be literally uncovered as the tangle of overgrown vegetation is hacked away. Deadly poisonous vipers lurk. Words in Latin and Italian must be decoded, as does a drawing of the grounds from the 1500s that Daphne finds coated with filth in her room.

When summarized, all this may sound like a Gothic melodrama. It's Lappin's skill as a writer, however, that makes the story perfectly plausible, its world quite real, grounded in the excellent concreteness of her prose. The voice of Daphne's telling has an authentic 1920s quality. Consider this passage chosen at random: "I found the professor standing at the parapet of the terrace, surveying the park, where we could see three young men industriously at work under Manu's supervision, hacking at the ivy with axes and scythes. Finestone looked like one of the workmen himself, for he was wearing blue overalls which starkly set off the gingery color of his beard..."

The qualities that unite the Chinese boxes of the novel may be found in Daphne's theory of signatures:

> We are constantly immersed in a network of signs and symbols whose meaning eludes us, but which, if only we could read them, would reveal every detail of our past and even predict our future. Like anticipatory echoes, they tingle in our consciousness, building a crescendo until the event they herald becomes fully manifest.

The challenge is to attain "a stimulated, heightened attention" that allows us to read them. Throughout the novel Daphne gathers a disparate collection of objects she knows are signatures, though she is exasperated by her inability to fathom their meaning—cigarette ends, a doll's head, a swatch of cloth, a pearl button. At the novel's climax, she experiences a thrill of illumination. She grasps the underlying design: "It all made perfect sense." The pleasure for the reader is joining with Daphne as she reaches that crescendo.

[Note: *Signatures in Stone* was the 2014 overall winner Daphne du Maurier Award for Excellence in Mystery/ Suspense.]

## *Katherine's Wish*

The more Katherine Mansfield approaches death, the more she comes to life in Linda Lappin's *Katherine's Wish*. That's not to say that she isn't a vivid character from the very first paragraphs of the novel, in 1918, on a train pulling its way through a blizzard, trapped in a compartment "pervaded by the sickening smell of mothballs, perspiration, and wet galoshes," taking "short, tremulous breaths to keep herself from coughing." This initial image of her on a frantic journey to Mediterranean sun, in pain, immersed in white, in coffin-like aloneness, is emblematic of her condition and the struggles she will face throughout the next four years in a desperate and futile effort to stay alive.

The novel's second paragraph introduces Katherine's thoughts  about the two people most important to her— her servile, smitten companion Ida Constance Baker, tagging along since their New Zealand girlhoods, and her self-absorbed, philandering husband, John Middleton Murry. She longs for Murry's closeness but endures the many absences he excuses first by War Office and later by editorial duties and financial hardship. Ida, on the other hand, is an annoying burden and a welcome respite, both suffocating and essential in her constant hovering.

Many others populate the novel, from the famous D.H. Lawrence and Virginia Woolf to the lesser known, such as Chekhov translator S.S. Koreliansky, Lady Ottoline, and P.D. Ousepensky, as well as Katherine's wealthy, distant father, two of her relatives, Murry's mistresses, and more.

Unlike the characters of most novels, these people existed as historical presences, and Lappin spent nearly two decades researching and writing *Katherine's Wish*. The dangers of writing a novel of this sort are many. All the information found in letters and diaries and documents could overwhelm the author with scholarship, resulting in a dry rendition of facts. Because the central characters are known to some extent to readers, the work could end up as a costume drama, parasitic in exploiting preconceptions and ready-made situations.

Lappin avoids these pitfalls by the strengths of her writing—the rhythms of her prose and the convincing specificity and vividness of the details. The interiors of the many rooms and the exteriors of the many landscapes are described with a cinematic richness: "This cool, wet August had plumped the blackberries on the bushes along the garden wall. She could almost taste their tartness with her eyes, but the leaves of the willows were edged in brown …"

A test for some readers will be Lappin's ability to create original portrayals of Woolf and Lawrence, a fresh way of seeing people whose identities are almost clichés. She does, as in this meeting between Katherine and Woolf:

> Conversations with Virginia were agonizingly slow to ignite. One had to break through the cocoon of isolation Virginia spun around herself, with her perfect demeanor, her flawless chitchat, even those ludicrous hats and dresses she wore were a deterrent to keeping others from coming too close.

But most crucial is the evocation of Katherine's consumption, the painful stages of her dying, her struggles for survival, her growing debilitation. Lappin reveals the spots on the lungs, the dysentery and fevers, the "ominous heaving rumble" of her coughing. Ultimately, she makes us care about a woman from literary history who has been dead for more than eighty years. Readers will share Katherine's wish that she could live forever. Lappin's achievement is to succeed where medicine failed and, through her words, give Katherine Mansfield ongoing life.

# Rabbit's Door

*I can't claim to have known John Updike, though I have read so many of his books over the years it feels to me that I did. My only personal contact with him was his offering of a series of versions of a sonnet, from the handwritten origi-nal draft on the back of an envelope to proofs before actual publication in* The New Yorker. *These were reproduced for a special issue of* The Literary Review *called "Poems and Sources," edited by Thomas E. Kennedy. Updike sent cover messages typed on postcards with a manual typewriter. He wanted all the originals returned, and I wondered what his extensive his filing system must have been like, how many rooms and cabinets it filled. My own brief association with Philip Roth also connected me with Updike, considering how often they were compared as rising young American writers and eventually as representatives of an aging gen-eration. Although I wrote this piece long before this col-lection's introductory essay, James T. Farrell also appears.*

> "The closet is in the living room and only opens
> half way, since the television set is in front of it."

That image has stayed with me from the first time I read *Rabbit, Run* in 1960, the year of its publication. It and the Angstrom's cluttered, rundown apartment typified confinement and frustration, life's inadequacies, all the things that don't function properly, everything you can't access. The detail bothered me then and still does.

Yet so much of my life in 1960 was different from Harry

Angstrom's. Challenged by sub-average height and sub-average coordination, I had never been a high school basketball star. While local newspapers trumpeted Rabbit's exploits, I was just an anonymous stringer phoning in game reports. And while Rabbit—all glory past—was struggling as a used car salesman for his father-in-law, I was a first-year graduate student, hoping my future lay ahead.

Still, I was enduring student poverty, pooling spaghetti leftovers with neighbors and living in one quarter of an army surplus tin hut. Married student housing. A tight space with a concrete floor, a metal kitchen unit, and no inside walls, just partitions. At the back of my mind, I feared my life would go wrong, expectations thwarted, nothing but defeat ahead, a door that wouldn't open.

## Updike and Rabbit

What drew me to John Updike then was the certainty that—despite his success at age 27, a publication list already beyond my fantasies—he too knew only a sliver of good fortune separated him from Harry Angstrom. Rabbit *c'est moi*.

As the obituary in *The Economist* put it: "Rabbit was so real that he might have been Mr Updike himself, had the hawk-nosed novelist not been saved by becoming a famous writer instead."

The Rabbit fate lurks out there for all of us. And sometimes even fame isn't enough.

## Updike and Roth

Born a year apart (1932 and 1933) publishing recognized work when barely into their twenties, touted as the future of American writing, eventually handicapped as contenders for the Nobel Prize, John Updike and Philip Roth made an unlikely pair. Their styles and their entire approaches to writing were so different. Coincidentally, I was a student of Roth's in 1960 and reading both *Goodbye, Columbus* and *Rabbit, Run*. As they have for so many others, they've been linked for me ever since.

But while Roth—when he settled into the novels of his mature phase—looked inward, with postmodern probing of his identities through the doppelganger Nathan Zuckerman and characters called Philip Roth, I never had the sense that Updike was exploring his own angst. Even if he was, the traumas and tribulations of his characters seemed their own, not autobiographical projections, but rather alter egos of his imagination, the way most writers create the people in their fictions.

Both men wrote about sex abundantly. (A mutual friend once told me Roth offered him money from the *Portnoy's Complaint* royalties because he was "the world's richest pornographer.") But it's hard to conceive of an Updike male masturbating into his family's liver dinner. The fervent couplings of his characters represent societal norms during the 20th century's decades of sexual liberation.

As they entered their seventies, both writers address the aging process, Roth more focused on impending death, Updike on nostalgia for lost powers and lost opportunities. Ironically, Roth was the man with serious health problems—including peritonitis and quintuple-bypass surgery—yet Updike is the dead one.

## The Way We Live Now

Because he looks outward, I associate John Updike with the great Victorian novelists who offered panoramic views of their own societies. There's an important differ- ence. Omniscient novelists like Dickens, Thackeray, Trol- lope, and Eliot saw the web of complex connections that bound their characters, no person apart from the forces of his or her community. Trollope's *The Way We Live Now* could serve as a generic title for much of Victorian fiction.

Updike, a product of American emphasis on individu- alism, revealed the nature of his society through the strug- gles of just one person, a Rabbit Angstrom. Rabbit, despite all that makes him distinct, is one of us, the archetypal late 20th-century American whose life makes us aware of what was happening all around us, another way of revealing the way we life. As Updike himself wrote in an introduction to an edition of the collected tetralogy: "Rabbit was a ticket to the America all around me."

## Rabbit and Studs

Once teaching a novel course, I compared the then- existing three Rabbit novels (a time before *Rabbit at Rest*) and James T. Farrell's Studs Lonigan trilogy—*Young Lonigan*, *The Young Manhood of Studs Lonigan*, and *Judgment Day*. Farrell is largely forgotten these days, but paperbacks of his prolific output were drug store staples when I was a teenager. I read everything I could get my hands on. Perhaps it was the occasional sex scenes—furtive and vague, but that was the only thing available in the era before Updike and Roth.

Studs was equally disappointed with his sexual initia- tion and infrequent subsequent encounters. But Studs was disappointed with just about everything in his life. Farrell followed the patterns of literary naturalism, his pathetic character crushed by his fate. Studs never had a chance. Of course, his novels were set in the middle of the Depression.

Rabbit became an adult in post-World War II America. He had, eventually, a house, a car, appliances, a wife, and a number of extramarital lovers. All that would have been beyond Studs wildest dreams. Yet Rabbit was never satisfied. He wasn't a victim of fate, rather the product of his own actions and choices and inadequacies.

In that belief, Updike shares an approach with another, quite different religious writer, Flannery O'Connor. Her stories and short novels portray Southern eccentrics, often comic in their ignorance. But, like Updike's Rabbit, they miss the point of what is important in human existence, what our living should be all about. In an O'Connor story, that insight is out in the open, the point of it all. In the Rabbit novels, it's usually implicit, though this passage says it all.

Shortly before the middle of *Rabbit, Run*, Rabbit brings Ruth, his lover, to a cliff overlooking their city:

> The city stretches from the dollhouse rows at the base of the park through a blurred broad belly of flowerpot red patched with tar roofs and twinkling cars and ends as a rose tiny in the mist that hangs above the distant river. Gas tanks glimmer in this smoke. Suburbs lie like scarves in it. But the city is huge in the middle view, and he opens his lips as if to force the lips of his soul to receive the taste of the truth about it, as if truth were a secret in such low solution that only immensity can give us a sensible taste. Air dries his mouth.

Here is Updike's lyric eye for visual details—he studied art before writing. But Rabbit in his Eucharistic longing seeks a more profound truth beyond the vivid physicality of his surroundings, one he never finds.

In his church-going Protestantism and his personal belief, Updike was a rarity for American writers of his and later generations. Many have forgotten that in the late 1960 and early 70s when the majority of writers and poets were on the front line of protest—burning draft cards and, in some cases, poems—Updike supported the war. Yet because he was such a good writer and, to all appearances, such a good man, few held it against him. If he didn't save us, he certainly enlightened us.

Like Harry Angstrom, John Updike is dead. The best Rabbit could do was beat a kid in a one-on-one basketball contest before his mistreated heart gave way. Updike accomplished infinitely more. Let us hope that he saw his life as fulfilled as do we who celebrate his work.

# Biblical Uncertainties

*Aviya Kusher and I exchanged only a few sentences when she was a visiting writer at a MFA residency. We had in common being students in the Iowa Writers' Workshop, years apart, and dealing with English translations of the Bible, though my involvement was far more basic. Like many who heard her talk and then read, I felt compelled to order her book at my first opportunity and, in my case, to write about it.*

I came to Aviya Kushner's *The Grammar of God* well prepared, having, a month before the book was published, heard her talk about her arduous ten-year writing process. When I first learned of her topic, Biblical translation, I expected a discussion of the typical complexities of rendering a work in a language other than its original. But she began her talk with a riveting revelation. Kushner, having grown up in a Hebrew-speaking home in an Orthodox community not far from New York City, did not encounter an English version of the Bible until her late twenties. From the opening verses of Genesis, Kushner was shocked by the many variations from the Hebrew version, the inaccuracies.

Kushner was introduced to the Old Testament in English when she took Marilynne Robinson's Bible as literature course while an MFA student at the University of Iowa. That led her to an immersion in research, including gathering a number of English translations and long conversations with Robinson. That prize-winning novelist, and author of works on Christian belief, convinced a reluctant Kushner to develop her master's thesis into a book that unites family tales with scholarship. Kushner now teaches as a member of the creative writing faculty at Chicago's Columbia College.

The challenge for Kushner lay in finding a way to organize years of notes and ideas into a coherent presentation, finally choosing a topical organization, with chapters on subjects such as creation, love, man, and law. While the alliteration of "grammar" and "God" makes for a catchy title, the work also explores matters of etymology and philology. The result has been greeted with much praise, the poet and translator Robert Pinsky calling the book "a passionate, illuminating essay about meaning itself."

The question of meaning is essential when a work in one language is rendered in another. Of course, the limitations of translation have been discussed many times. *Zeteo,* recently considered, for example, a futile attempt to render in French the idiomatic English poetry of Philip Larkin—Larkin's word choices, rhythms, and sensibility. When the translation of a poem is unable to capture its qualities, that's an aesthetic failure. But when the Bible goes wrong in another language, the problematic consequences can be theological, political, legal, and moral. The results often have involved—literally—matters of life and death, if not entire belief systems rooted in a fundamental misapprehension.

Take the King James wording of the very opening of Genesis: "In the beginning God created the heaven and the earth. And the earth was without form, and void, and darkness was upon the face of the deep." Kushner explains that the other best-known English versions also make two distinct sentences of what was just one in Hebrew. This syntactical separation changes an important distinction of what existed when. The King James has the earth "without form, and void" after it was created. The Hebrew single sentence suggests the unformed was the raw material used in the creation.

But more crucial is the tense of the first Biblical verb. English readers for centuries have assumed God "created the heaven, and the earth," with the implication that the process was over and done with. Such an assumption gives comfort to the deniers of evolution and those who believe Adam and Eve shared the planet with dinosaurs, even building museums to display pseudoscientific "proofs." But what if the verb tense was that of an ongoing present, as in several more recent translations—when God "began to create heaven and earth"? Such a process is ongoing and accommodates continuous evolutionary development.

The Hebrew original doesn't settle the issue, mainly because the Hebrew language didn't employ the diacritical markings that function as vowels until the eighth century. These indicate tense, but they are lacking in the original Genesis text. Subsequent markings added to post-vowel versions of the Hebrew Bible in the Middle Ages have been based on guesswork. And, for example, a dash below leads to a very different meaning from a dot above.

Beyond matters of tense, Kushner offers a more definitive example of a questionable translation with what the English version renders as "Thou shalt not kill." That's one of what our culture considers the Ten Commandments, laws so essential to some believers that they want to replicate the stone tablets in public spaces. Nowhere does the Hebrew Bible identify them with the harsh title of commandments. Rather, it suggests a more benign identifier, such as the ten sayings. But back to "not kill." Kushner points out that the Biblical Hebrew word—*lirtzoach*—clearly means murder and that another word—*laharog*—means kills. The Hebrew Bible uses the former; therefore, "do not murder." Forbidding murder is very different from forbidding killing. War and self-defense serve as two examples where killing is not an un-Godly transgression.

In fact, the Bible is replete with examples of killing of enemies in war. Cain murdering Abel is another matter. But even some stories of slaughtered enemies can be troubling, at least to me.

Coincidentally, decades before Aviya Kushner came to Iowa for an MFA, I taught the Bible as literature on that campus. *The College Bible,* compiled from the King James version, served as the text for half a semester of a sophomore core literature course.

Kushner arrived knowing the Hebrew Bible inside and out, having read extensively in the writings of important commentators of many centuries, and having engaged in many family dinner-table debates about the subject. I knew almost nothing beyond second-hand Bible stories acquired here and there, and a week or two in my own college survey of English lit.

As I young instructor, I walked into that core lit classroom in what was known as the Bible Belt for the first time expecting every student to be steeped in Biblical lore from years of Midwestern Sunday schooling. They would expose and humiliate me. How wrong I was. They knew nothing. Well, perhaps some of the same few tales I did before I devoted many hours to teaching preparation. I came to enjoy discussing the Bible as literature and getting the students to engage with a number of narratives, good stories all with an engaging cast of characters.

Now that I've read Kushner, I wonder how much damage I did to those young Midwestern minds. But I excuse myself by rationalizing *The College Bible* was a literary text to be analyzed for just what was on the page, even if that page was riddled with translation inaccuracies. I taught the Bible as if it were a work of fiction like *The Odyssey* and *Much Ado about Nothing*.

Yet on a number of occasions I was unable to separate fiction from fact, particularly when slaughters were involved. Take the Amalekites "utterly destroyed" by King Saul under the orders of the prophet Samuel or the slaughter of the Hivites, whose prince, Sechem, seduced Jacob's daughter Dinah and wished to marry her. Dinah was the sister of Joseph and his brethren. The brothers claimed to agree to allow the marriage if the Hivites converted to Judaism and all the men became circumcised. That was a ruse. While the males were helpless with painful post-op recovery, the Hebrews slaughtered them.

But the—let's call it—tribal massacre that troubled me most involved how David dealt with the children of Ammon after his army conquered the city of Rabbah. I still have disturbed marginal notes in my copy of *The College Bible*. According to the King James' version, 2 Samuel 12-13 has it that David first took the spoils of the city and then "... he brought forth the people that were therein, and put them under saws, and under harrows of iron, and under axes of iron, and made them pass through the brickkiln ..."

Kushner led me to seek out other translations. Not only do some soften the brutality, they turn the vicious death sentence into hard labor. For example, The New International Version has is as: "consigning them to labor with saws and with iron picks and axes, and he made them work at brickmaking." There's a world of difference between being hacked with an axe and incinerated in a brick kiln oven and being forced to toil in brick making. The latter way, putting the conquered to arduous work, is just one more example of enslavement of the defeated.

I asked Kushner about this discrepancy, but— perhaps because after her talk others were swarming the lectern with their own questions—she didn't provide an answer beyond a nod and smile.

She does write in her introduction about the limits of translation: "Translation means that the translator has picked one word above all the others: one winner, with all the finalists gone from the page forever." She writes this in reference to the grammatical, syntactical, and philological debates about meaning that obsessed generation after generation of Hebrew scholars. Unlike literary translators, they weren't content to settle for a single winner.

But while the story of the children of Ammon does suggest a zero-sum translation choice rather than a complexity of nuances, it could be that the original Hebrew itself was equivocal.

Regardless of what happened to the children of Ammon—just one translation ambiguity among thousands—the conclusive point of *The Grammar of God* has to be that the Hebrew Bible—the Old Testament—cannot be considered a final and conclusive document, set in stone along with the larger-than-life Ten Commandments statuary.

Of course, the Hebrew Bible that served as the foundation of Kusher's comparisons is itself the result of one alternative from among the number that existed as scripture among the Hebrew communities spread throughout the ancient world. These texts can differ greatly in some respects, and one version, the Masoretic of the fifth through seventh centuries, became the basis of Kushner's Bible, though that's not a subject she goes into.

Like heaven and earth the Hebrew Bible should not be considered "created" but rather a document once and forever "being created."

**Works Cited**

Brennan Breed. "What Are the Earliest Versions and Translations of the Bible?" *Bible Odyssey*.

Aviya Kushner. *The Grammar of God: A Journey into the Words and Worlds of the Bible*. New York: Spiegel & Grau, 2015.

*The College Bible*. New York: Appleton-Century Crofts, Inc., 1938.

# Books Everywhere

The clerk at the Iowa City post office was overjoyed to see me. I had driven from New Jersey in an underpowered Volkswagen bug, one of those Spartan first-generation models with no gas gauge and certainly no room for eight boxes of books. It barely accommodated clothing and a few pots and pans. So, envisioning the post office of a town I had never seen as a structure much like a railroad terminal with a vast storage area, I mailed the boxes to myself care of general delivery. But when I walked into a small building, there they were, stacked right behind the poor clerk, cramping his space.

When I returned to New Jersey five years later in a new VW and two toddlers in the back seat, family clothing stuffed into the front hood luggage space, plastic bags under foot, even more boxes of books were shadowing my route east in the hands of the U.S. Postal Service. As much as I had scrimped for food and shelter and eventually diapers and formula, I managed to acquire several hundred more, the pages of my education.

I began acquiring books as a teenager with a massive ignorance of literary history—the canon of the time, which writers were important, those who must be read. My choices came from browsing the paperback racks at a local drug store in our small town, just whims, attracted by a title, a cover, a blurb about the story. I still have some of those books, their pages yellowed and brittle. In fact, I just stood up from my keyboard, walked two steps to a shelf and pulled down Aldous Huxley's *Eyeless in Gaza*, a "complete and unabridged" Bantam book that cost me all of fifty cents. The back cover touts another work from Bantam, Walt Sheldon's *Trouble of a Star*, "The Novel of the Korean War." As far I can remember, I passed that one up. But I read a lot of Huxley and still have the evidence. What I don't have is any Erskine Caldwell, *Tobacco Road* or *God's Little Acre*. Most likely they were stolen in a high school study hall where my sex-starved classmates never got beyond certain dog-eared passages.

Our teachers certainly didn't instill a taste for good writing, not with their spoon-feeding of *A Tale of Two Cities* and daily quizzes with questions like, "What color dress was Lucy Manette wearing when such and such happened?" I swore never to read another Dickens and didn't until graduate school, when I became a fan and even signed up for a Dickens seminar. A stack of his works was in one of the boxes shipped back to New Jersey. If I swivel my chair, I can look right at them.

A number of books from my undergraduate years are stashed around our house too. If I went downstairs now, I could go right to the copies of Plato, Aristotle, Machiavelli, Hobbes, Locke, Rousseau, and others from a political theory course, still snug one next to the other.

As far as I can recall, I built my first bookcase in college. In those days very few of us could afford cars, and I remember carrying boards on my shoulder across town from a lumber yard to the fraternity house, then borrowing a hammer to nail them together. In houses and apartments over the years, too strapped to buy finished products, I constructed bookshelves from floor to ceiling and stuffed them as soon as the paint was dry. In a condo closet I installed metal strips with slots for metal braces for six rows of shelves that I invariably overloaded and would hear crash down several times a year despite my wife's warnings not to pile all those books again. Where else could I put them?

In our present house, one we've lived in for a dozen years [twenty now], I do have professionally built-in shelves on a wall in this small room I use as an office. That's where I keep my British lit, the Huxleys and the Dickens and the rest, all those other writers I read to complete various degrees and just to know. The office also has a closet with a set of prefab bookcases with an unspecified mixture of books, a couple of shelves housing my own printed writings, out of sight behind a closed door. Other books sit stacked on the closet floor until I figure out what to do with them, not to mention even more heaped on cabinets in the office, on the floor, and even on a small easy chair, where – at this moment – one of our cats is happily snoring atop them.

The built-in shelves in the room we call the library, where we also watch TV, hold another random mixture, including many books written by friends and some there just because of aesthetic bindings and dust jackets. As Anthony Powell said in the title of one of the A *Dance to the Music of Time* series, Books Do Furnish a Room. I'll find almost all of my American lit two rows deep behind cabinet doors under those open shelves. In yet another closet off the library, sit my political theory, philosophy, history, European and Asian lit – dozens by Dostoevski and Tolstoy and Sartre and Camus. And who knows what else?

The basement contains more books shoved into three pressed-wood cases that came as kits and have followed me around to several residences over a few decades. Mainly, they're books that I've never sorted into more orderly categories. In fact, other than my Brit lit and American lit, most of my books are housed helter-skelter despite my resolve to create coherence when we moved into this house. But, as I've noted, that was twelve years ago. I'm ready to admit it will never happen, even after I've run up and down stairs, opened doors, gotten on hands and knees in search of a book I really need at that very moment and have no idea where I put.

And then there are my wife's books. But I won't mention them.

For quite I while I've been telling myself that I have to get the library habit, check out a book, read it, and return it when done. But I rarely follow though. It's so easy to click through amazon.com or wander into a local bookstore. And then I've got all these friends who publish books. How can I not buy and own them? What are friends for?

It's not that I haven't given away books. Boxes of them, in fact. When I retired from full-time teaching and cleaned out my department office, I stacked hundreds on a wide ledge in a stairwell leading up to our floor. Except for a handful of defunct 1970s literary magazines, all were taken by someone else, now cluttering their homes. And I've been to some of those homes, books piled from floor to ceiling, barely a space to walk though.

Perhaps because I'm old and am certain to die sooner than later, my wife occasionally asks, "What's going to happen to all these books?" The subtext is that they're almost all worthless paperbacks of titles that exist by the thousands or by authors no one reads any more. A new edition of *Eyeless in Gaza* will be out in October 2009. As of today, the old one is 712,518 in sales at amazon. My copy, with the greatest luck, might end up as one of those one-cent specials on abebooks.com.

I'm certainly never going to read *Eyeless in Gaza* again in this lifetime. For that matter, it's very unlikely that I'll reread *Moby Dick*, *Women in Love*, *Barchester Towers*, or even *Our Mutual Friend*. For that matter, with all the people I know turning out new books, I'll never find time to read any of those old books in the days I have left. So much for my one-time fantasy of completing all of Trollope.

So why do I have them all, so many that if I shipped them again, the Iowa City post office would probably bar the door? Why don't I do my survivors a favor and get rid of them now? I can't. It would break my heart. They're a fundamental part of my life, the RNA of where I've been and how I got here. Vital to what's made me me. I can just look at a shelf and recall hours of pleasure and discovery. In many cases, plots, characters, scenes, words, ideas still linger in my memory. But even when I've forgotten everything, as is the case with *Eyeless in Gaza*, the spine of that paperback brings back the sense of my teenage reading, baby steps out of ignorance, initiation into a world so much larger than my conscribed self. These books envelop me in the abundance of the world and remind me of all that matters. It won't be till I go that they go.

# Rooms of Their Lives: Where British Author Lived and Wrote

*Of course, I didn't know these writers—with one exception, not personally; but their books surround me, literally on shelves in my office and deep in my literary memory.*

Over numerous trips to Britain, I've gone out of my way to make pilgrimages to authors' homes, driving for hours to small country towns or walking miles through London neighborhoods to view the sites of their lives. After all, these were the men and woman whose writings have become the source my teaching profession—English Literature. I owe them my career, my livelihood, and my excuse to travel to such a green and pleasant land. For all my travels, I barely made a dent in the list of possibilities. So many authors, so little time. What I did take away from those visits was hardly scholarly, mostly trivia, odd juxtapositions of the minutiae of place with the creations of genius.

### Shakespeare

Where else to begin? And the tourists all know it, of course. His birthplace in Stratford is the most visited of all English authors' homes, busloads clogging the highways from London on their way to a town of souvenir shops and half-timbered Tudor buildings glutted with human and vehicular traffic. But that's in the high season. I saw the birthplace on a raw, grey February day, almost alone in the house, a few other people several rooms behind, unseen, their footsteps echoing. Wood creaked. Walls tilted. It was a rather pleasant house, I recall. Roomy for England, not a bad place to spend a sixteenth-century boyhood. But it gave me no clues to Lear, no hints of Hamlet. Where they came from was a mystery far beyond habitat.

Years later in a summer, the town overflowing, we sat in a park by the Royal Shakespeare Theatre—not far from the church were the Bard's dust lies entombed—and watched an orange cat scurry up the bank from the Avon with its jaws clamped on a large rat. A rat behind the arras. The plunge of a dagger. Polonius dead. Ophelia mad. Laertes enraged. Did vermin roam the birthplace, infesting the imagination?

## Samuel Johnson

Samuel Johnson, overweight and gout-ridden, lived in London at 17 Gough Square, set back just a short distance from today's heavily trafficked Fleet Street. It's fitting that the author-editor of The Rambler, The Adventurer, The Idler, three eighteenth-century periodicals, should have his memorial a stone's throw from the [now former] center of twentieth-century English journalism. It's a narrow house of many stories with a very steep stairway. Straining my own way upward, I wondered how a man of the Great Lexicographer's heft and infirmities could negotiate them day after day of his life in the city.

Yet Johnson must have made the journey from ground floor to the top of his house many times, for he wrote of the virtues of garrets in No. 117 of The Rambler, Tuesday, April 30, 1751: "... and nothing is plainer, than that he who towers in the fifth story, is whirled through more space by every circumrotation, than another that grovels upon the ground-floor."

That's Johnson on paper. Did he huff and groan and bemoan the actual ascent to the heights? Or, conscious of his legend, of Boswell's recording ear at his side, did he put on a good show, offering epigrammatic gems with each pained step as he clutched the banister?

## Thomas Hardy

The thatched cottage of Hardy's boyhood is situated far from a city, in the Dorset village of Higher Bockhampton, on a narrow countryside lane several miles from Dorchester, his fictional Casterbridge. I remember it surrounded by vegetation—vines and shrubs and flowers—but with a view of fields from the second story. Using the dwelling in his fiction, Hardy wrote that the walls "were for the most part covered with creepers, though they were rather beaten back from the doorway." When we arrived, the only visitors at the time, perhaps of the entire day, the caretaker was mowing the lawn outside the front door. He explained that under an arrangement with The National Trust, which owned the building, he lived there rent-free in exchange for such maintenance duties. And he supplemented his income through sales of Hardy paperbacks displayed on a table in the living room.

That room was by any standards tiny for its function. It couldn't have been much more than eight by ten. Yet it was, as the caretaker explained, the setting for a village dance in an early Hardy novel, *Under the Greenwood Tree*. I bought a copy, a 25 pence paperback, intrigued by the notion of a party gathered in such cramped space, much less jumping around to country fiddles. Yet one of the chapters describing the event is called "They Dance more Wildly," four heavy men stripping off their coats reeling with "flapping shirt-sleeves," the ladies' earrings "now flung themselves wildly about, turning violent summersaults." Perhaps Dorset people in the late nineteenth century were much smaller than they are today, even more miniscule than Queen Victoria.

At the back of the cottage, in the little kitchen, a wooden ladder, two fixed beams and ten or so cross steps, led up through a trapdoor into the bedroom Hardy shared with his brother, the only way up or down. Dr. Johnson could never have maneuvered it. Perhaps the ladder became emblematic of Hardy's social and artistic climb. He ended up London—famous. But his heart is buried in Dorset, just ashes of the rest of him lying in Westminster Abbey's Poet's Corner.

## William Wordsworth

When Wordsworth lived there, Dove Cottage, Grasmere, in the Lake District was even further in the English hinterlands than Higher Bockhampton, not the holiday haven it is today, with its dozens of hotels and charming B&Bs, boat trips the length of Lake Windermere. Though most of the Cumbrian mountains are less than one thousand feet, dwarfish compared to, say, Mont Blanc, people found their ruggedness forbidding until Wordworth and his fellow Romantics convinced the world of their sublimity: "The mountain's outline and its steady form/ Gives a pure grandeur, and its presence shapes / The measures and the prospect of the soul / To majesty . . ."

Coleridge, Walter Scott, Thomas De Quincey, Charles and Mary Lamb, Robert Southey, sister Dorothy—they all congregated about the small cottage where Wordsworth lived during his most creative years. It was certainly a humble place, with white limewashed walls and slate floors on the ground level, but what struck me most was the contrast of the functional accommodations in most rooms with that of the children. There, the walls were covered floor to ceiling with sheets of newspaper, shellacked over, a feeble protection from what must have been fierce winter winds. Poor shivering babes they must have been, while below poets huddled by the fire and spoke of beauty.

When the conversation broke up at midnight, the young Coleridge long ago would begin his midnight walk over the stark and empty hills back to his lodgings in Keswick. It's fifteen miles between Grasmere and Keswick. How did he do it night after night? Did he fortify himself with laudanum before setting out?

Now, a brick museum outside the cottage displays letters, manuscripts, memorabilia, all explained in affectionate detail by the guide speaking in a Cumbrian dialect, who might be called a Wordsworth savant, an autodidact. A local man, without the academic certification expected of someone with such expertise, he clearly had devoted himself to the poet's life, at least to the years at Dove Cottage. Perhaps it was his pure dedication, perhaps the children's room, or perhaps the glass-cased handwriting of a major poet in his youth—but I found myself moved by the visit.

Of course, the Wordsworth who became an official figure was a bit of a stick. His longtime home Rydal Mount (1817-1850), just down the road from Grasmere, sits many roomed on a hillside overlooking the lake. But, compared with Dove Cottage, it's a stuffy place, smacking of self-satisfaction. Wordsworth did plant a field of daffodils for his daughter Dora. And that's a step up from newsprint wallpaper. But, would we think better of the poet if he had died early in the cottage, his life was destroyed by TB, drowning, madness, or addiction?

## D. H. Lawrence

Like the guide at the Dove Cottage museum, the middle-aged woman in charge of Lawrence's birthplace in Eastwood lacked formal schooling, yet was immersed in the writer's life. A month or so before we saw the house, she had literally retraced the footsteps Lawrence described in *Twilight in Italy*. With great pride, she showed us the guestbook signatures of famous visitors like Tennessee Williams. And she revealed that many Eastwood old-timers resented D.H. for the way he treated his father on the page; they had great affection for the elder Lawrence, thought him a fine man.

The brick house belied my expectation of a collier's home from *Sons and Lovers*, as did the town itself. Of course, this was many decades after Lawrence's boyhood, but the house was bright and comfortable, not dingy and soot-covered, the town neat and orderly, not choked with coal dust. Just a brief walk away lay a surrounding countryside of green hills and wide meadows.

Primed by months of reading, we had driven directly from landing at Heathrow in the midst of a heat wave, the temperature in the 90s, the sun sultry. Foolishly, we walked out beyond the streets several hundred yards to the gates of the coalmine. It wasn't particularly ugly; it didn't dominate the town. Even during our long, slow return through the town to our car, dizzy with heat, humidity, and jetlag, we found no signs of filth or squalor.

Nowhere had we seen Lawrence's Eastwood: "So, the actual conditions of the Bottoms [the blocks of miners' dwellings], that was so well built and that looked so nice, were quite unsavory because people must live in the kitchen, and the kitchens opened on to that nasty alley of ash-pits." Not an ash-pit in sight.

## John Keats

I confess only the vaguest memory of Keats' home in Hampstead, probably because that day we lost our bearings on the Heath, trudging for what seemed like hours toward a church steeple I felt sure was a Hampstead landmark, only to end up several miles away in Highgate. What I do recall of the house on Wentworth Place was a sense of an official dwelling, almost neoclassical in its order, certainly not a repository of bloody handerchiefs. And it was difficult to imagine frail Keats out at night indulging in the trendy wine bars and four-star restaurants of this upscale neighborhood.

Years later, walking in Rome, we came upon the Spanish Steps and looked up at the windows of the room where Keats died. But they were repairing the steps themselves, the entire area roped off from the public. We couldn't get closer.

## Jane Austen

If Keats and today's Hampstead are a mismatch, Jane Austen and Chawton, Hampshire, still fit perfectly. The town is a quiet, tranquil place, neat and orderly on the surface, "a remarkably pretty village," in her words.

The house Jane lived in from 1809 until shortly before in 1817 death in Winchester is a large square, many-chimneyed building of red brick her family called a cottage despite its six-bedrooms. She wrote in a parlor with a large table and rows of miniatures over the fireplace on floral wallpaper, no rug on the plank floor, the space sparsely furnished like her bedroom on the floor above.

The place is archetypal Georgian, clean lines, fenced garden, and an absence of clutter. Yet an underbelly of gossip and social maneuvering wouldn't be surprising in a town like this, possibly a mother or two scheming to marry off daughters. At least, that's the feel one gets, even though those daughters are all most likely out on their own in London, meeting potential mates in pubs or on the Internet. And many are probably earning good money in the media, unfazed by the notion of spinsterhood.

The house is located on what was called the Winchester Road, separated from the roadway by only a thin strip of grass. It was to Winchester that Jane was taken in her final illness, to a city with what passed for better medical attention. She died in a rented room. I passed the building once, noticing the plaque on the brick on my way to car park, walking close enough to read the words.

### Charles Dickens

I've managed to see two of Dickens' homes, the one in London at 48 Doughty Street in Bloomsbury and the one overlooking the Channel in Broadstairs, Kent. If the Austen house was spare and Georgian, Dickens' were cluttered and Victorian, the rooms packed with things, not the mess of, say, Krook's rag and bottle shop in Bleak House, but abundantly furnished, like his eccentrically populated novels, dozens of characters all bound by a tangle of coincidence. The Dickens world is fraught with details, almost every detail a clue to a mystery. He liked to pack things in and saw patterns in the plethora.

### Thomas Carlyle

One afternoon on the long drive south from Edinburgh, I noticed a sign for Ecclefechan, a name that had stayed with me for decades, ever since I encountered it in a sophomore survey course—the Scottish birthplace of Thomas Carlyle. Given its lowland location in an undistinguished landscape, I doubt that it attracts many visitors. It's Lockerbie, less than ten miles to the northwest that— sadly—has name recognition in our time. And Carlyle, unlike Austen and Dickens, does not inspire readers' emotional attachment. The house itself was small and ordinary, offering no signs of the man or his mind. Given his temperament and drive for the heroic, Carlyle must have been eager to get out of that town and head for the metropolis. His heart certainly isn't buried there. Coming from a place called Ecclefechan probably marked him for life, turning him into a churlish curmudgeon, fighting with his wife, denigrating the times he lived in.

### Penelope Lively

The title of her first serious novel, *The Road to Lichfield*, refers to Dr. Johnson's birthplace. He too was a young man from the country who made it big in the big town, though his wisdom is hardly as inflammatory as Carlyle's. Although she has achieved her own success as a contemporary novelist and story writer, winner of a Booker Prize, Penelope Lively is not yet one of the major names of Eng Lit. She's still adding to her oeuvre.

In the early 70s, I lived next to her for sixth months in

the Oxfordshire village of Church Hanborough. I rented an accommodation in the Tithe Barn on one side of the churchyard, while she and her family lived in the Old Rectory Farmhouse on another. At the time, she was writing novels for adolescents, historical tales set in the period when the Cotswolds' affluence came from wool production rather than tourism. This was my first trip out of the U.S., and she quickly reoriented my sense of historical time on my third day in the village. The church, she told me, dated back to the eleventh century. The Tithe Barn existed on maps from the early 1500s. But the pub was "new," she said, only eighteenth century.

I remember one afternoon standing with her over a heap of old roof slates, worn thin by almost six centuries of weather. They had been pulled from the barn when the new owner, an artist living in London, replaced them with fresh square slates. She was exasperated that he had just given them to a man who asked if he could cart them away like debris.

Back then I did not know how good a writer she is because she had not even begun her adult fiction. But reading her books years later, I understand the source of her deep concern with time and place.

## The Brontës

At first, Haworth—the second most-visited English authors' home—disappointed me. The narrow streets and the low grey granite buildings were perfect for the mood I expected. But the town was nowhere as remote as I had expected. The Haworth of my imagination sat alone, surrounded by empty miles of heath. But standing on the main street, looking at the valley to the east, I could see the row houses of a nearby town with their tiny walled yards. It felt cramped, dense.

We booked one of the few rooms in the Black Bull Inn, right in the center of things, the site of brother Branwell's dissipation. When I requested a room key, the barmaid gave me a look of disbelief that I would ask for such a thing. The doors did not lock. Perhaps to give access and egress to the ghosts? I didn't want to know. (I still have the receipt from April 16, 1972: bed, breakfast, and service charge for four — £7.48.)

The Parsonage, off behind the main street, did look exactly like a home for the Brontës—bleak, severe, rows of tombstones in the front yard. Large rooks cawed endlessly from high, bare treetops. But those trees did not exist in the sisters' day. Then the graveyard slabs were totally unsheltered. Of the house's interior, what struck me most was the narrow little settee that Emily died on after completing her daily chores and feeding the dog. It was her dog, but she was known to beat him when she thought he misbehaved. Timid as she was in the world outside, at home within the family she exerted a fierce presence.

I discovered the true Brontë country on the moor behind the Parsonage, out past crescents of new housing with names like Heathcliffe Court and Catherine Lane. There on a landscape of thick, dense foliage, shades of green, contoured far out to the horizon, my shoes tangled in undergrowth. Eager for an encompassing vista, I sought the peaks of rises, only to find more rises ahead and to the right and left, no way of taking in the whole. After an hour of struggling with vegetation, only a short distance from the village, I found myself tired, ready to turn around, amazed that those tubercular sisters could hike miles out and back with such weak lungs, only days from their dying.

Perhaps in a pure aesthetic world, the works of the great British writers would exist only on the page, anonymous as medieval sculptures and cathedrals, to be appreciated totally for themselves, untainted by our knowledge of the creators behind them. But the human in us seeks the human in them—their chairs and beds and writing desks, the pictures on their walls, the dishes they ate from, the rooms of their lives.

# *Creative Minds and Mental States*

In our house we often cite the late psychologist Albert Ellis, who is reported to have said, "Everybody is fucking crazy." That seems right to us. But the other night I read a claim that people of higher intelligence, especially creative types, are more prone to mental disturbances than the average person. I've encountered similar studies over the years. Could it be that creatives are even fucking crazier?

It's difficult for me to judge because, by far, most of the people I associate with and email daily are writers—from those I spent time with when getting my own MFA, to those I edit, those I write to, those who are close friends, and those who are my MFA students. These writers range from eager novices to winners of prizes and Guggenheim and National Endowment for the Arts grants. Their books overflow my shelves. Beyond writers I know well are those I've met briefly through an introduction or a brief exchange, major names in the literary world. I suppose I'm one or two degrees of separation from a good percentage of the planet's authors. Other than a few nervous tics, a tendency to obsess over rejections, and occasional evenings when they're in their cups, writers all seem pretty normal to me, no different from the average person.

But what do I know? I recall sitting at a dining-hall table with a group of MFA colleagues and students with everyone discussing their medications for depression and anxiety. Wellbutrin seemed to be a favorite for the age group because it doesn't suppress the libido. Then again, millions of non-writers swallow SSRIs every morning. They're probably not as prone to sharing.

The study I read last night claimed a greater prevalence of bipolar disorders for the creative. It may have been referring, among others, to research by Nancy Andreasen at the University of Iowa. When I was there, she held a position as an assistant professor of English specializing in John Donne. But she thought better and went on to earn a medical degree and eventually hold a chair of psychiatry, still at Iowa. Taking advantage of her dual background, she tested various faculty members in the MFA writing program and concluded bipolarity and depression were rife among them. She probably would have come to the same conclusion if she had extended her subjects to MFA students at the time, many of whom would become well-known writers and writing teachers themselves.

Here's one of her conclusions:

> Many personality characteristics of creative people...make them more vulnerable, including openness to new experiences, a tolerance for ambiguity, and an approach to life and the world that is relatively free of preconceptions. This flexibility permits them to perceive things in a fresh and novel way, which is an important basis for creativity. But it also means that their inner world is complex, ambiguous, and filled with shades of gray rather than black and white. It is a world filled with many questions and few easy answers. While less creative people can quickly respond to situations based on what they have been told by people in authority—parents, teachers, pastors, rabbis, or priests—the creative person lives in a more fluid and nebulous world. He or she may have to con-

front criticism or rejection for being too question-
ing, or too unconventional. Such traits can lead to
feelings of depression or social alienation. A highly original person may seem odd or strange to others. Too much openness means living on the edge.
Sometimes the person may drop over the edge...
into depression, mania, or perhaps schizophrenia.

Note that Andreasen, to her surprise, found no schizophrenia among her writer subjects.

On a number of occasions that had nothing to do with
creativity, I've visited mental wards and witnessed very
bizarre behaviors. I've even written about them in short
stories. To my knowledge, none of those patients were writers; but I do know about Robert Lowell, John Berryman,
Sylvia Plath, and others who went off the deep end. Was
that because they wrote or because of malfunctioning syn-
apses? Were the patients I saw suppressed creatives who
had dropped over the edge?

After many conversations, exchanges, and interactions
with writers, even years in their company, I'm still amazed
when reading their work—fiction, poetry, or nonfiction—and
trying to reconcile the products of their imagination with the
person who chatted about a movie or music or politics or a
trivial or serious personal issue, from a crashed laptop to a
broken marriage. They speak like other people, though with
a somewhat larger vocabulary and more wit. But on the page
they reveal a different identity, often a magical transformation
into something worthy of wonder. They exist as the person
across the table and as the writer who expresses the complexity
and ambiguity of his or her inner world.

While *bipolar* may be an excessive term for the great
majority of the writers I know, bifurcated minds may serve

as a general explanation of how writers differ from the typical person. Although I've asked a few other writers—who concur—and a few non-writers about my premise, I'm afraid I'll have to rely on myself as a research subject, the only stream of consciousness I really know.

I suppose a certain degree of bifurcation takes place in all human minds between what people do and say on the surface of their lives and what goes on in the monologues of their thoughts—daydreams, dreams, replays, what could have been, what shouldn't have been, all those running commentaries that are difficult to turn off but can be put on pause through absorption in a game or film or TV show. Yet when the games and shows have ended, in the darkness of night, the head on the pillow is probably teeming with an inner reality. If that reality is painful, some resort to substances, from the soporific to the mind-altering.

The bifurcation of the writer's mind—while often like that of all people—morphs into a different realm through an outlet into an alternative reality: fiction or poem or drama or essay, a distinct actuality transformed from the confines of the brain to objectification on a page or a screen. It becomes a public statement available to anyone who chooses to pick it up or watch it.

The written piece may be very autobiographical, especially to anyone who knows the author. Yet even though the root information may be factual, words and rhythms and strategies of presentation have transformed what may have happened into something new and different. The result is not a report but much more an enhancement and interpretation. And even when the world written about is far from that of the writer in place or time or circumstance, the piece is still existentially autobiographical because it is the product of the authorial mind revealing the imperatives of that mind.

While the ongoing concerns and narratives of the typical mind are free flowing and unshaped, the writer's mind is often composing—seeking the right words and organization and structure to turn the raw material into some form of literature.

There's a platitude writers share when one experiences an unpleasantness, whether it be lost luggage or a failed marriage: Well, it's something to write about. And it is. In fact, just about everything, all that happens or is witnessed or is felt is material. Finding the outlet and refining the delivery are what distinguishes the writer's mind from that of the great majority.

For some people—say teenagers after a devastating romance—what they call poetry serves as an outlet for their misery. And it isn't only adolescents. Once when I was shopping for a small appliance at Sears, the salesman sensed something about me, perhaps the gray beard, and asked if I taught literature. When I admitted that I did, he reached into a wallet and pulled out a sheet of yellowed paper folded so many times it was about to split apart. He asked me to read a poem he had written about a woman who had broken his heart. I did, stifling my inclination to suggest revised lines, and muttered something complimentary, though useless to assuage his suffering.

Still, writing as an emotional outlet is different from writing to produce what might be considered a form of art, with awareness of the need for craft and revision, an absorption into technique that overpowers the initial raw emotion that led to the need to express in the first place. The Sears salesman didn't want advice on making a better poem. He wanted psychic relief.

Of course, preoccupation with the dynamics of craft is another kind of release and relief. It allows an objectification of what might have been a source of tears and sleepless nights. Or just a need to lose oneself in the shaping of words, the making of another reality.

If nothing else, writing is a harmless alternative to a lethal weapon in manifesting our fucking craziness.

**Work Cited:**

Nancy C. Andreasen. *The Creative Brain: The Science of Genius.* Plume, 2006.

# Will Computers Write Literary Fiction?

Would it matter to readers of the future whether a work of fiction was written by a person or by a robot if they weren't aware of the difference? I'm thinking mainly of what is designated as "literary fiction." Much genre fiction is inherently formulaic, variations on basic patterns that fans of the specific genre expect and want. In fact, they most likely would be disappointed, if not disturbed, by unusual shifts from the predictable.

One successful romance writer, Lori Devoti, lists five scenes every such novel should have: 1) the meeting of the couple that ends with some conflict, 2) their awareness of what they share, still ending with conflict, 3) their physical attraction and yet more conflict, 4) dramatization of their emotional commitment, and 5) a sacrifice for love that outweighs any conflicts. "So, if it's a formula," Devoti claims, "so is life."

A writer of literary fiction would disagree, instead affirming Tolstoy's, "All happy families are alike; each unhappy family is unhappy in its own way." It may be that even happy families differ, but literary fiction is not about them, unless it reveals the unease beneath the surface.

Could a computer programs write romance novels? They already have produced acceptable news items, business reports, and similar pieces. Such outcomes involve entering concrete information, like the score of a football game and the earnings of a corporation and processing them through a fixed organizational structure. A romance novel that emulates a standard development pattern must provide new information such as the characters' names and backstories, where they live, the specific nature of their conflicts, etc. Can such details be incorporated into a program? Probably, eventually, because they are just variations on the expected—different scores, different earnings, different conflicts. Good literary fiction, in contrast, lacks fixed patterns and predetermined expectations.

Writing in *Business Insider* in late 2014, Joshua Barrie, a UK tech reporter, claims, "Computers are writing novels — and getting better at it." And he wonders, "if the creative professions are safer than the administrative or processing professions" from the progress of artificial intelligence (AI). Still, how good must a computer-generated novel be to make the thousands of storywriters and novelists writhe in nightmares?

Alan Turning, Barrie reports, back in 1950 already came up with a measure for literature with a variation of his famous Turing Test. He posits two stages, a soft test in which human readers can't tell it's not human generated, and a hard test in which human readers not only can't tell it's not human generated, but will actually purchase it.

The "breakout hit" computer-written novel of 2013, Nick Montfort's *World Clock*, failed the test of getting Barrie to rush to his nearest Waterstone's for a copy. The algorithms programmed by Montfort, a digital media professor at MIT, turned out passages such as these:

> It is now exactly 05:00 in Samarkand. In some ramshackle dwelling a person who is called Gang, who is on the small side, reads an entirely made-up word on a box of breakfast cereal. He turns entirely around.

> It is now right about 18:01 in Matamoros, In some dim yet decent structure a man named Tao, who is no larger or smaller than one would expect, reads a tiny numeric code from a recipe clipping. He smiles a tiny smile.

And several more such paragraphs of similar information. The pattern is clear. Time and place, what kind of building, character name, character size, something read, a gesture made. The limitations of the tales of Gang and Tao and others might give literary fiction writers sighs of relief.

A few years before, in 2008, Russia's SPb publishing company shipped bookstores *True Love*, a 320-page work created by IT professionals to retell Tolstoi's *Anna Karenina* in the style of Haruki Murakami. Here's a representative passage: "Kitty couldn't fall asleep for a long time. Her nerves were strained as two tight strings, and even a glass of hot wine, that Vronsky made her drink, did not help her. Lying in bed she kept going over and over that monstrous scene at the meadow."

Such sentences emulate familiar story telling, but *True Love* can be considered a sport. The Tolstoi original already exists, and Murakami's stylistic tics can be broken down into 0s and 1s. Essentially, with the plot a given and the presentational method predetermined, that novel is a merging of two sets of knowns rather than a creation of something fully new.

Since both *True Love* and *World Clock*, however, the Google AI program Alpha Go defeated the world's champion Go player Lee Sedol in a five-game match. Apparently, that was a huge leap in harnessing computer potential to realize a form of exceptionally, superhumanly creative strategic analysis.

The game of Go, which I know little about, apparently is exponentially more complex than chess. AI specialists consider the recent achievement of Alpha Go far more significant than IBM's Watson's groundbreaking defeat of chess master Gary Kasparov in 1997. A computational Everest has been climbed because the number of the number of possible games of Go far exceeds the number of atoms in the observable universe and is more than a googol times larger than the possibilities of chess.

So many possibilities, so many choices. I'm reminded of a bit of wisdom offered by George P. Elliott (*Among the Dangs, Parktilden Village*), who explained the creative challenge: "What makes fiction writing so difficult are all the decisions the writer faces." That's seen in every word choice, in every arrangement of syntax, in every character detail, in every item of backstory, in every transition, in every step of plot; in short, in everything.

If Alpha Go can master the challenge of more than all the atoms, could an equivalent AI program first master romance novels and then literary fiction? Could mastering an extraordinarily complex game translate into mastering an extraordinarily complex creative task? Will fiction writers go the way of assembly line welders before, say, 2025, replaced not by robots but by highly inventive algorithms? Artificial intelligence already has outperformed human abilities such as making medical diagnoses more accurately than physicians and allowing cars to drive themselves more safely than people. What about a computer program that turns out literary fiction?

Headlines in March 2016, perhaps influenced by the halo of the AI Go triumph, announced that an AI-composed novel came close to achieving a literary distinction in Japan. Here's one, "A Japanese A.I. Wrote a Novel, Almost Wins Literary Award," specifically the Nikkei Hoshi award. Titled *The Day a Computer Writes a Novel*, the work seems to be a self-conscious metafiction. The final sentence, the only one translated into English at the time, gathered many intrigued comments: "The computer, placing priority on the pursuit of its own joy, stopped working for humans." Beyond the alliterative syntax, the sentence embodies fears of our species becoming superfluous.

To the relief of many, it turns out the headline was overblown false news. The novel had a great deal of human help, not unlike a term paper cobbled together from plagiarized passages. According to a professor who worked on the project, the human input amounted to about 80 percent of the endeavor.

Jacob Brogan reports in *Slate*, citing the Japanese publication *Ashai Shimbum*, that the research team first wrote a novel and then broke it down into its component parts to feed into the AI process that rearranged the words, phases, characters, and plot to come up with a story parallel to the human-written original. In short, AI manipulated source material rather than truly creating. I'm reminded of the Russian Tolstoi-Murakimi construction. Really creating without prompts and templates may be even more of a challenge than winning at Go.

Recently I came across James Salter's *The Art of Fiction*, a brief book compiling three lectures he gave as the first Kapnick Foundation Distinguished Writer-in-Residency at the University of Virginia. Salter, who died at age 89 in 2015, was nothing if not a writer of literary novels and short stories, much praised for the lyric precision of his prose. In the lectures he discusses how he became a writer, how he wrote, and how he learned from other writers.

Most significant to me was his sense of the standards for good writing and how hard it is to meet those standards. He notes that Gustav Flaubert turned out 4,500 pages of drafts for what became a 300-page masterpiece, *Madame Bovary*, endlessly revising and at times producing only a page a week in search of *le mot juste*.

Salter emphasizes the importance of the sentence, how an author's distinct voice, his or her way of telling, comes though in sequences of words that lead a sentence "to bloom in the reader's mind." He cites Isaac Babel, who said, "...there was no iron that could piece the human heart with as much force as a period put in just the right place."

Salter echoes George P. Elliott when he says writing a novel is such a complicated process because it's not possible to hold all the details in your head. "You have to keep track of many things, even apart from who is where and what has happened," he explains. "Inevitably there are notes tacked to the wall or taped to an outline." Today such notes may be digital, off in a corner of a computer screen. The main thing, Salter emphasizes, is selecting from and finding an order for all those specifics.

Throughout all the hours it takes to create a novel, writing is not confined to a specific time or a specific place. "You do it elsewhere," Salter explains, "carrying the book with you. The book is your companion, you have it in your mind all the time, running through it, alert for links to it."

Having written a bit of fiction myself and having fiction writer friends who talk about their process, I can't but agree with all that Salter says about the all-encompassing absorption of writing fiction. Unlike a computer, our imaginations won't power down.

But back to computer-written books. Phil Parker, a chaired professor of marketing at Insead: The Business School for the World, reports that once two or three years have been devoted to developing the right algorithms, a book can be generated in twenty minutes. He claims, going one step beyond Lori Devoti:

> We created a system which we think mimics the human mind... The truth is, if you step back far enough, all of literature is highly formulaic, not just romance novels. Some of the genres are so formulaic that the publishers of those genres tell the potential writers how to write the books themselves.

I can't help by compare that twenty-minute span with the full decade several of my novelist friends devoted to a single work, resulting in grants, awards, and enthusiastic reviews. That makes me wonder how Lee Sodel, that world champion Go player, must feel after multiple defeats by Alpha Go. But then I wonder about sentences that pierce the human heart.

Even if a future algorithm actually produces fiction capable of passing the Turning Tests of convincing readers and finding buyers, even going beyond bestseller lists to win National Book Awards and Man Booker Prizes, I suspect the James Salters of the world won't stop writing novels and stories because for them the process, as long and as demanding as it may be, matters much more than the product. Can an algorithm enjoy the satisfaction of achieving a sentence that blooms or a single word that feels exactly right?

## Sources:

Joshua Barrie. "Computers Are Writing Novels: Read a Few Samples Here." *Business Insider* November 27, 2014.

Jacob Brogan. "An A.I. Competed for a Literary Prize, but Humans Still Did the Real Work." Slate March 25, 2016.

Lori Devoti, "Five Scenes Every Romance Novel Needs." *The How to Write Shop* July 30, 2012.

Google Official Blog. "AlphaGo: using machine learning to master the ancient game of Go." January 27, 2016.

Adam Popescu. "Why Write Your Own Book When an Algorithm Can Do It For You." *Read Write* January 15, 2013.

James Salter. *The Art of Fiction*. University of Virginia Press, 2016.

Walter Cummins"># Existentialism and Story Writing

Sarah Bakewell's *The Existentialist Café: Freedom, Being, and Apricot Cocktails*, led me to revisit the details of my lifelong inclination toward existentialism and reaffirmed my decision to make it my equivalent of a religion, or—more accurately—belief system. Bakewell organizes her examination of existentialism around the lives of the central thinkers, with tantalizing tidbits about their friendships and fallings out, their wives and lovers, their personal tensions over evolving and conflicting theories. But her approach offers far more than revelations of inside gossip—who said what and did what, who turned against whom, who felt betrayed. Biography is inseparable from existentialist thinking: the ways we live, choose, and shape our lives are fundamental to our understanding of the nature of human existence.

In many ways, the existentialists remade the approach to philosophy by personalizing it so profoundly. For them, philosophical systems are not a set of theories "out there," like mathematical formulas, to be grasped by intellects independent of personal experience, detached from the emotions and behaviors of that person. Instead, the existentialists believed, philosophies are revealed in our interactions with the world around us. Rather than being "out there," philosophies come from within, inseparable from our actions and our choices.

Because some of the best-known existentialists—e.g.,

Jean-Paul Sartre, Simone de Beauvoir, Albert Camus—
wrote novels, stories, plays, biographies, they saw human
lives in terms of narratives based on character creation, dramatic questions, and the responses of characters to those
questions. Whether or not those characters were aware of
existentialist ideas, they could not help but demonstrate
them in their actions—like all of us. Beyond my life choices
at times of uncertainly and trauma, I've chosen to manifest my own existentialist leanings through story writing,
engaged with fictional characters—people—confronted
with their own need to act and choose.

Bakewell discovered her own existentialist inclinations
when, at sixteen, she made a choice to spend birthday present money on a copy of Sartre's *Nausea* because a blurb
described it as, "a novel of the alienation of personality
and the mystery of being." Although she didn't know what
alienation meant, she found the novel capturing her young
state of being, leading her to skip school and decide she
wanted to study philosophy. I was a few years older, around
twenty and clearly alienated, when I experienced the illumination that I'd been an existentialist all along, much like
Monsieur Jourdain's discovery that he had been speaking
prose all his life without realizing it. The book I imprinted
on was Albert Camus' *The Myth of Sisyphus*, my original
paperback filled with affirmative markings. Yes! yes! The
book told me so much about my own inclinations to question and break from the preconditions that would, if I let
them, determine my niche in the world. It explained the
flounderings of my young Angst. I had the satisfaction of
knowing I wasn't alone in my uncertainties and that someone had elucidated my condition.

Bakewell did pursue her philosophical studies when

the fascination of reading Martin Heidegger led her to enter a PhD program, though she dropped out to, instead, become a writer of nonfiction books, primarily biographies, and teach creative writing at an Oxford college. (She received that National Book Critics Circle Award for *How to Live: A Life of Montaigne*.) She tells the stories of actual people, in a sense turning them into characters.

I knew I didn't have the depth of mind to be a philosopher. But at 22, I realized I didn't want to end up spending my life as a corporate executive. Although I did not know the concept then, I instinctively understood that I would have devoted decades retreating into a version of what Sartre, in *Being and Nothingness*, called "*mauvaise foi*" (bad faith). He uses the example of a waiter gliding through a dining room fully absorbed in the act of being a waiter; that is, playing a role and leaving his own identity behind. Of course, some bad faith is necessary to function in the world, at least to interact with a salesclerk or chat at a cocktail party. But to do so constantly is to deny one's essential freedom and fail to truly live. Instead, as the existentialists urge, we should confront painful uncertainties and seek to be authentic.

My seeking took me to grad school and a creative writing program. But with many open elective credits I gravitated to courses related to the history of ideas, including an independent study in existentialism with the then head of the philosophy department. It's clearly my own limitations, but like Jean-Paul Sartre and Simone de Beauvoir's bafflement when they first read a French translation of Heidegger's "What Is Metaphysis?" I understood little of the English versions of his convoluted sentences. Bakewell, in contrast, demonstrates an ability to explain theories with concise lucidity. If only Bakewell's book had been around then to teach me. But at least I knew I had decided well in not trying to be a philosopher.

The acclaim Bakewell's book has received pleases me because my previous recent encounters with opinions about existentialism have been dismissive. I took them personally: they were rejecting me, my beliefs. For example on "Philosophy Bites," an online series of brief discussions that address various philosophers, Dame Mary Warnock of the Oxford faculty dismissed Sartre as "not an original thinker" and a bad writer who was just "a minor offshoot of German phenomenology." She did praise him for opening "our eyes to the fact that moral philosophy could be an exciting and totally relevant subject."

Yet her overall assessment gives him a minor role in the history of thought. John Gerassi, who, like Warnock and the novelist Iris Murdoch, wrote books about Sartre, explains their diminishment of Sartre this way: "... both Iris Murdoch and Mary Warnock put Sartre down for not playing the game the way they do, that is, by using logic as a philosophical method rather than descriptions."

For me in my youth and still today, and apparently for Sarah Bakewell, it's this reliance on descriptions—placing the narratives of our human interactions with the world at the core of what matters—that makes existentialism so appealing. Formal logic may be lacking, but experience is met head on. That's what people in stories do.

In my openly existentialist twenties, I wrote a number of grad school essays on existentialist themes, my first titled "Men of Absurdity," in which I reread *The Myth of Sisyphus* to consider Camus's theories, his novels, Sartre's *Nausea*, Par Lagerkvist, and Dostoevsky. I was, of course, revealing a personal quest, uncertain whether I would make it as a student or a writer, with no idea what would happen next if I did manage to finish the degree. Having rejected the societal givens the majority assumed were certainties, I was seeking identity and authenticity, though all I saw ahead were unknowns and the threat of inadequacy. Still, I lived in the moment. Despite the pressures and anxieties, it was great fun.

In the Absurdity essay I composed a month just before my twenty-fifth birthday, I wrote, reflecting on Camus, "The lucid man must avoid illusion, false hope or false despair; for his lucidity is his greatest gift. [...] He realizes that the answers to his most urgent questions are beyond him. He must ignore what he cannot know and base his life on the evidence of his lucidity."

For Camus, we are launched into a plethora of meaningless phenomena, and that it's up to us to find our own moorings by trying to make some sense out of all that "stuff," something to grab onto. We can't rely on a set of givens to do that work for us, no predetermined set of beliefs or values to guide our lives. While we may borrow from them, we—essentially—have to create ourselves, though our choices shaping who we are and will become.

Camus' central concept to explain our frustrated hope for meaning is the Absurd. The term Absurd is often interpreted as meaning the world outside of us is meaningless. But Camus states that we can't and don't know enough about the world to come to such a conclusion. The Absurd is a condition rather than a concrete. It's our human situation of yearning to understand the world around us—the phenomena—and the impossibility of getting answers. The world may be teeming with meaning, but—if so—such meaning is not accessible to us. All that theologians, philosophers, and scientists have tried to explain, they are just groping. We humans have no choice but to create our own individual realities because we can't exist without some assumption of order, even though that assumption is only a functional heuristic, a temporary crutch to help us maneuver through the day. Our real challenge is to face head on the fact of all that we will never know and like Meursault at the end of *The Stranger* open ourselves "to the tender indifference of the world."

Camus ends up reversing the opening question of *The Myth of Sisyphus*—whether to choose suicide rather than live a meaningless life—to conclude the exact opposite, that life without meaning is the greatest reason for living. Each experience can be enjoyed for itself and life can be accepted fully. For him the quantity of experiences is what matters. The bad faith of plodding through daily life is a waste of our years. We should savor what each day brings, alert to the richness of the moment, even when that moment is a trial. Our days are all we have.

But how does enjoying each experience relate to story writing? In *Sisyphus* Camus recommends that in the absence of a life that coheres into a single shaped significance our best option is to collect experiences, the more the better. It's perhaps a version of the ironic bumper sticker: "Whoever dies with the most toys wins." But Camus isn't being ironic. Experiences are all we have. Don't expect meaning and immerse in the doing to do all that you can.

Part of my own drive for experiences has been travel, the challenge and pleasure of attempting to immerse in a range of places and environments. Often I take a few minutes to look at the photos and listings of realtor windows, trying to envision what it would be like to actually live in that place.

Writing stories is a much less expensive extension of actual travel, the opportunity to—through imagination and words on a screen—inhabit many lives and many worlds and conceive what it would be like to cope with many personal crises. In a secondary sense, so are reading, watching, overhearing, and observing.

If, as Bakewell argues, biography is essential—the choices that shape our lives—stories allow us to engage with a multiplicity of biographies beyond our own. Of course, the great majority who are not story writers get their stories second hand through the books they read, the plays they attend, and the movies and TV shows they watch. They seek gossip and scandal about the lives of others, neighbors and celebrities. While most people do not accept Camus' notion of the Absurd, they live as if they do, eager to deny it, spending much of their time entranced by stories that—unlike "real" life—make some sense of the world. Still, it's better to be an active existential creator than a passive receiver, especially if that passivity serves as an escape of truly living and ends up being a form of bad faith.

While the act of writing stories can be frustrating, failure a real and frequent possibility, even the unsuccessful drafts offer an opportunity to immerse in other lives. I've turned well over one hundred stories, engaging in many worlds and many people and many dramatic uncertainties. Even stories from decades ago are vivid in my memory, a multiplicity of intense vicarious experiences that are my own. I suppose my bumper sticker could read, "Whoever writes the most stories wins."

**Walter Cummins** has published seven short story collections—*Witness, Where We Live, Local Music, The End of the Circle, The Lost Ones, Habitat: Stories of Bent Realism,* and *Telling Stories: Old and New.* More than 125 of his stories, as well as memoirs, essays, and reviews, have appeared in magazines such as *Kansas Quarterly, Virginia Quarterly Review, New Letters, Under the Sun, Confrontation, Bellevue Literary Review, Serving House Journal, Connecticut Review, The Laurel Review, Other Voices, Georgetown Review, Contrary, Sonora Review, Abiko Quarterly, Weber Studies, Midwest Quarterly, Zeteo, West Branch, South Carolina Review, Crosscurrents, Crescent Review, The MacGuffin,* in book collections, and on the Web. With Thomas E. Kennedy, he founded Serving House Books, an outlet for novels, memoirs, and story, poetry, and essay collections. For more than twenty years, he was editor of *The Literary Review.*